# MIND POWER

This book explores the mysteries of the human brain and the potential of the mind. The peculiarities and infinitude of the mind have been a theme for research for scientists and philosophers alike, for centuries.

This volume presents the unanswered and highly convoluted questions and hypotheses surrounding the human mind in a simplified way. It examines the binaries of religion and science, god and nature, and emotions and intelligence through a philosophical lens to posit that the relationships between cognition, belief, nature, and science are what we understand and infer based on our surroundings and how much we are willing to think, learn, and introspect.

This book will be of interest to students of philosophy, psychology, science, popular science, psychoanalysis, cognitive studies, and mental health. It will also appeal to general readers.

**Ethirajan Rathakrishnan** is Professor of Aerospace Engineering at the Indian Institute of Technology Kanpur, India.

# Mind Power
The Sixth Sense

**Ethirajan Rathakrishnan**

Routledge
Taylor & Francis Group

LONDON AND NEW YORK

First published 2023
by Routledge
4 Park Square, Milton Park, Abingdon, Oxon OX14 4RN

and by Routledge
605 Third Avenue, New York, NY 10158

*Routledge is an imprint of the Taylor & Francis Group, an informa business*

© 2023 Ethirajan Rathakrishnan

The right of Ethirajan Rathakrishnan to be identified as author of this work has been asserted in accordance with sections 77 and 78 of the Copyright, Designs and Patents Act 1988.

*British Library Cataloguing-in-Publication Data*
A catalogue record for this book is available from the British Library

ISBN: 978-1-032-22486-2 (hbk)
ISBN: 978-1-032-23065-8 (pbk)
ISBN: 978-1-003-27552-7 (ebk)

DOI: 10.4324/9781003275527

Typeset in Times New Roman
by Apex CoVantage, LLC

This book is dedicated to my parents,
Mr. Thammanur Shunmugam Ethirajan and
Mrs. Aandaal Ethirajan

# Contents

# Prologue

This book discusses the sixth sense or intuition, often attributed only to humans. In the following chapters, I have attempted to explore what intuition or sixth sense is and authenticate hypotheses around it using numerous evidences existing in nature and the natural phenomena which show that others in nature might possess intuitive powers as well.

But are there ways through which the power of the mind can be aroused? This compelling question is analysed in the book by using examples from science, philosophy, and spirituality. Additionally, it deliberates on various practices, superstitions, and beliefs about the mind, God, spirituality, and human agency in the world. I would like to emphasize that the contents of this book are based purely on ideas and beliefs of the author, especially regarding the power and capabilities of the mind. Researchers and scientists are conducting numerous tests and are making breakthroughs to understand the mind and how it works, but there are aspects and mysteries which are yet to be mapped fully. To understand these phenomena, we can rely on the knowledge we possess in various disciplines and our powers of deduction. The ways and means projected for tapping into the mind's powers in this book are the author's perceptions and based on his experience, and they should in no way be deemed universal.

It is expected that this book will be of some value to the readers in analysing and understanding their mind.

Ethirajan Rathakrishnan

# 1   Introduction

## 1.1  Energy Potential of Mind

One of the fundamental questions the human race has had is if it is possible to quantify the energy potential of the mind. The mind is a wondrous organ, it is the source of not only limitless emotion but also multidimensional intellectual ability, including rational thinking as well as foolishness. Many great scientists and philosophers throughout history have tried to study the mind in order to know its true potential and limits; however, the true potential of the mind is still quite shrouded in mystery. It should be emphasized that the power or energy embedded in the mind is the basis for all activities of the living species, beginning from the one-sense plant kingdom to the six-sense humans. In our everyday life, we observe that we experience many emotions. A keen observation clearly suggests that there is some controller in the body that controls all these sensations. This key power controller is termed mind. Another feature that we should note and analyse is the effect of the activities of the mind. A group of people having a flair for reasoning out anything before accepting it are recognized as people equipped with scientific spirit. Those people who cannot be understood by the common public possess some features which make them immerse in eternal pleasure; they mostly remain silent and lead a detached life. These people are recognized as saints by the world. The power of the mind is the basis of the attitude of these groups. Therefore, there is enough reason to think that the energy of the mind has a variety of role to play. From the activities of the species, such as animals and birds, it is evident that they too have power of intuition to distinguish between good and bad, similar to human. This raises question on our perception that only human beings have the sixth sense or intuitive or logical thinking.

The brain, which enables us to learn, store memories, or perceive things made scientists and philosophers to undertake the study to understand the mind. But this task was not easy since the brain has remained the most mysterious organ to study and know for quite some time in modern scientific history. It is quite fitting to state that the wisdom to understand the power and potential of our mind has to come from the mind itself. This makes our minds

DOI: 10.4324/9781003275527-1

as the diamond tool which cuts and shapes other diamonds. It is an interesting puzzle, to see and understand that the knowledge necessary to understand the potential of the mind has to come from something which is powerful enough to assess it and to which it belongs. This puzzle is quite bewildering—for our brain to possess the power to judge an event and infer the consequences. Philosophers keep probing to understand the relation between the mind and body for centuries.

The field of artificial intelligence (AI) that focuses on the problem of the intellectual ability of human brain has developed to a large extent.

In one of these AI experiments, it was found that the nerve fibres called "C-fibres" in the brain can shoot information to the spinal cord, which in turn can transmit the message to the part of the brain which activates the energy embedded in the brain. However, the reason for the agonising flash of pain is still a black box.

Curiosity to learn the intellectual ability of the brain bridged the border between philosophy and science which scientists and *philosophers* alike keep pondering laboriously over. Not so long ago, many sections of thinkers were also of the opinion that brain does not have the sensations, such as pain. The debates around questions of the mind have come a long way due to people floating these hypotheses and contrarian viewpoints, but the puzzle is far from being solved.

Information about the ability of the brain and its intellectual and rational power keep floating; however, the doubt about gaining full understanding of this issue has remained a black box in both intellectual and philosophical spheres. However, the ability of the brain that enabled the scientists to solve many problems associated with survival and reproduction kept the hope of the world alive that it is possible to understand the power of the brain. But the search for finding a solution quantifying the power potential of the brain continues as a mystery even today.

Going a step further, one may ask—what does the phrase "power of the mind" mean? (Chronister, 2017). Is it its thinking ability, analysing power, intuition, something else, or the combination of all these? Thus far, no one has found a definitive answer for this either. The confusion is if we consider the ability to think as mind power, one would also assume that this is possible only when we are awake. However, what then does it mean to dream?

Are dreams a result of the thinking ability of the mind? How do we find answers to these questions? The reason why so many questions are raised when we try and consider what our minds are capable of is our desire to estimate its full potential. Though humankind has to its credit a large number of discoveries and inventions, in both theoretical and applied sciences, the power of the mind, which is responsible for these numerous scientific inventions and discoveries, is yet to be understood fully. The continuous evolution and invention of many theoretical applications to map and understand the brain justifies this.

Many studies have been and are being conducted all over the world to explore these questions. People have comprehended that the human intellect is irreplaceable. However, there is no sufficient data to authenticate this. Also, there are uncertainties and vagueness in the data, even in the available data, when it comes to human mind. The discipline based on human intellect called "knowledge management" was thus created. The human intellect (understanding) is the capability of a human mind to generalize experiences, to work with abstract terms, and to make conclusions from assumptions.

It is estimated (and this has garnered much attention in the scientific world) that even the most celebrated scientist of the modern world, Professor Albert Einstein, had used only a small fraction of his mind's power potential. The continuous study made on the structure of the Einstein's brain preserved in Princeton university is the evidence for this. Hence, it is natural to ask whether it is really possible to estimate the quantum of mind power and its quality? Although many theories, such as the one by Robert Pepperell (2018), exist, we have not even scratched the surface of this very convoluted problem. Philosophers, poets, and spiritualist have also pondered upon and written about mind and power. Saints like Thirumoolar and scientists like Joseph Murphy and many others all over the world have written about this question. Their efforts so far have not borne fruit, not in absolute terms.

The questions around the human mind or consciousness are shrouded in mystery, and because scientific research has not yet been able to understand how limitless is the power of the mind, scholars in theology, philosophy, history, and the sciences have tried to find answers elsewhere, they have studied the relationship between science and religion. Science and religion is a recognized field of study with dedicated journals, academicians, scholarly societies, and recurring conferences. Most of its authors, who are theologians, philosophers with an interest in science, or scientists with long-standing interests in religion (Stanford Encyclopedia of Philosophy Archive, 2017), have often compared mind power with the power of nature, the spiritual world, or the power of God.

## 1.2  Endless Effort

Humans have assumed for many centuries that the human mind is the most advanced and possesses something called the sixth sense. Defined simply, sixth sense is the intuition or the mind's capacity to infer one thing from another related piece of information. People blessed with a keen observation will not only suspect this definition but would also say that this inference or conclusion about the sixth sense has to be re-evaluated. Based on the theory that all species possess senses, humans had classified the living species into six groups: species with one sense, species with two senses, species with three senses, species with four senses, species with five senses, and species with six senses. Species such as trees, bushes, grass, and so on belonging to the plant kingdom were classified as those possessing only one sense; shells, snails, and the like were classified under species with two senses; ants and termites under three senses; crab and flying insects under four senses; and animals and birds under five senses. Only human were classified under six senses. It was believed that the sixth sense, namely the intuitive power, was a gift extended by nature only to mankind, putting them at the top of this hierarchy.

If we take a keen look at the movements of the world, we will realize that these demarcations and categories about the senses of living species can be questioned. If we assume that the sixth sense is a kind of intuitive wisdom which enables one to infer the consequences that may result from the events of deeds we observe or undergo, it is seen in nature that all living species, including the plant kingdom population, have this kind of intuitive power. For example, animals such as cattle (cow, goat, sheep, etc.) after grazing in the evening return to their respective shelters, without any guidance. Similarly, when cattle try to eat the crop grown in the farmlands, they are always on the alert of looking at the surroundings. If they spot anyone approaching the farm, they immediately run away and escape. This action of the cattle hints at their sense of self-preservation and intuitive thinking. Soon after spotting that someone is approaching that zone, it runs away from the farm to escape punishment.

This kind of feeling and the consequences implied are observed in trees and plants as well. When we observe and analyse these aspects in the world of living species, it is natural to question whether the so-called sixth sense is unique to humans alone? Thus, doubt about the truth or validity of these theories is nothing but natural.

All scientific inventions and discoveries are the result of the intuitive power of the sixth sense which the mind possesses. The power of the intuition relies on the power potential of the mind. As mentioned previously in this chapter, the discovery that scientists like Thomas Alva Edison and Albert Einstein, who contributed immensely to science and technology, used just a small fraction of the power potential of their mind was astounding to many. And if this is true, is it possible to quantify the full potential of mind power? Scientists, philosophers, and spiritual saints, such as Thirumoolar, Vallalar, and Bernard Shaw, who have thought or written about this question often concluded that it is impossible to estimate the power of the mind.

Thirumoolar attempted to quantify the power potential of the mind in his *Thirumandhiram*, a Tamil poetic work written either in the 6th century CE or post–10th century CE in India, which is the 10th of the 12 volumes of *Tirumurai*, the key texts of Saiva Siddhanta and the first known Tamil work to use the term. These poems question and ruminate on the extent of the mind's power, which he also visualizes through various metaphors and aphorisms, and declared that the supreme head which controls the mind possessing limitless power is God or the Almighty. The same supreme power has been referred to as nature by others. The third group, namely the philosophers, like Bertrand

Russell, a British philosopher, declared that God and nature, which control the mind power, are one and the same.

According to Russell, the following aspects are of primary importance: (i) Faith in the concept of God and immortality. Those who have faith in these believe that Jesus Christ is the best and the wisest. Also, they believe that adhering to these makes all our deeds relevant and meaningful. May be because it is a hypothetical or conceptual matter, Russell's views are somewhat vague. He says, "there is, it is true, a Modernist form of theism, according to which God is not omnipotent, but is doing His best, in spite of great difficulties". This view, although new in Christian thinking, is not new in the history of thought. It is, in fact, to be found in Plato. I do not think this view can be proved to be false. I think all that can be said is that there is no positive reason in its favour. In his writing on "Is There God", he concludes:

> There is no reason to believe any of the dogmas of traditional theology and, further, that there is no reason to wish that they were true. Man, in so far as he is not subject to natural forces, is free to work out his own destiny. The responsibility is his, and so is the opportunity.
>
> (Oppy and Pearce, 2021)

This question, which has boggled the minds of saints, atheists, and philosophers, has been answered in simple terms by a disciple of Bernard Shaw— "the extreme level of intelligence is *ignorance*". Those who try to get an answer to the limits of the human mind will be rendered silent if they find the answer. Or those, who find the answer to this question, cannot quench the thirst of the common man, who is eager to know the limit of the power potential of the mind.

## 1.3  Views of Science about Mind Power

We know that thermodynamics is a branch or discipline of applied science. Thermodynamics deals with energy and its change from one equilibrium state to another. Thermodynamics sees (treats) energy as heat. Further, it classifies the heat energy as mechanical, electrical, static, and magnetic energy. It also finds that the total energy potential after this classification has some portion of its energy content unclassified or un-understood. This portion of total energy which can neither be understood nor be utilized is termed internal energy. When we try to change one form of energy to another form, for any particular or specific application, it is impossible to convert all the available energy into a useful form and utilize it. Thus, during energy conversion from one form to another, some portion of the available energy is always left unconverted. This is called internal energy.

While designing work delivering machines, such as petrol, diesel, and steam engines, the designer aims to utilize the full potential of the fuel, such as gasoline, diesel, and coal by burning them. The thermal energy liberated in the combustion process is used for the working of these engines. Here the main focus of the designer is to bring out the full potential of these fuels. But despite their best efforts, 100% of the calorific potential of the fuel cannot be used. The portion of the energy content of the fuel, which cannot be utilized for work output, is referred to as internal energy. Also, it is stipulated by science that the total energy content of the universe is invariant. What science attempts to do is changing one form of some available energy to another form suitable for the operation of the devices designed and developed. Thus, science accepts that energy can neither be created nor be destroyed. This aspect—it is impossible to generate new energy or destroy the available energy—is often referred to as the power of nature by scientists, like Albert Einstein, and the power of God by the spiritual world. These conclusions of science have a direct relevance to the power of the mind, since the potential of the brain is responsible for this kind of scientific theories and their refinement. That is why it is perceived that the power potential of mind is limitless.

As per Pepperell (2018), for scientists, information is a fundamental property of nature. It is however perceived as the most fundamental property of nature by a few. Neuroscientists are of the view that information processing is the basis for the functioning of the brain. We read that "the brain is fundamentally an organ that manipulates information" and that brains are "information processing machines". Individual neurons are treated as information processing units, while neural firing patterns are converted into sequences of binary digits (1s and 0s) that encode *information*. Recent prominent theories claim *consciousness is identical with or results from certain kinds of information* structures or information processes in brains.

## 1.4  Philosophers' Views on Mind Power

Most of the philosophers have held that if mental states are something material, but not behavioural, then mental states are probably identical to internal states of the brain. Let us see the views of some well-known philosophers on mind power.

Plato argued that the mind and body are fundamentally different because the mind is rational, which means that examining the mind can lead to truth. In contrast to this, we cannot believe anything we experience via the senses, which are part of the body, because they can be tricked.

According to Descartes, the mind is an eternal device in a body that governs various activities such as spiritual that is abstract, scientific that is rational, imagination that is vivid, sensations, and desire.

According to Socrates, the mind and body are interrelated. This theory impressed Plato to the extent of realizing that the power potential of mind is made up of two modules: the part that governs the senses of feelings and the part that governs the scientific and spiritual ideas.

Presently, both scientists and philosophers agree that mind is something special and in all probability it is a power centre of the body in which it is hounded.

## 1.5  The Immense Power of Energy

Both the scientific world and the spiritual world accept that it is not possible to measure and quantify the great power of nature. A simple example to highlight this aspect is the power of an earthquake. An extremely huge mass of landscape is shaken by the power of an earthquake as if a mother swings her child in a cradle to make it sleep. Imagine the amount of energy required to jolt a huge portion of the earth.

Similarly, it is impossible to quantify the amount of energy contained within a cyclone, tornado, typhoon, tsunami, volcano, forest fire, thunder, and lightning. The spiritual world perceives this energy as the amalgamation of five elements: land, water, fire, wind, and space, all of them constituting the animate and inanimate things of the universe. The amalgamation of these five elements, which constitute everything, is referred to as the Godly Power by theists, as stated in the book *Tholkappiyam*, a Tamil grammar book (Puliyur Kesigan, 2012). *Tholkappiyam* is the first written record available to us to assess the views of the ancient Tamils regarding Murugan worship. It refers to Murugan as Ceyon, meaning youthful. *Tholkappiyam*, which is also the oldest available literary work in Tamil, has governed Tamil grammar.

It seems that there is a 3-yard slip for every 1-yard climb: by the time we feel that somehow the power has been understood, the human mind comes out with yet another new concept, which squashes our previous understanding of power and energy. As we saw, thermodynamics could be able to quantify the amount of energy to be added or removed from a system when it changes from one equilibrium state to another. But even before thermodynamics comes out with this information and summarizes its energy principle, another question is raised about the happenings during the transition from one equilibrium state to another, and the time for the completion of this change from one level to another. The consequence of these inquisitive questions is the birth of a new field, namely the science of heat transfer. Heat transfer (Rathakrishnan, 2012) addresses the issues of the transient state energy levels and the duration of the transition process, which thermodynamics could not answer. The pathos of this scientific evolution is that even before the science of heat transfer could evolve fully and get stabilized, another branch of energy science, namely quantum mechanics, was evolved (Griffiths and Schroeter, 2018; Rathakrishnan, 2015) answering the questions such as what are the forms of energy, how do they look like, and are these forms and arrangements of energy source stable. With the evolution of science leading to the birth of the field of thermodynamics, human mind started questioning the capability of thermodynamics to answer the state of the transition states while a source of energy changes from one equilibrium state to another. This kind of inquisitiveness is the natural tendency for a trained mind that is aware of the built-in power in it.

In Hindu philosophy, three deeds—creation, protection, and destruction—are embodied by the Gods Brahma, Vishnu, and Rudhran in India. In Western theology, creation and destruction are embodied in God and Demon, respectively.

The Shaiva and Vaishnava sects in India believe Shiva and Vishnu, respectively, as their primary deities. But these primary deities are essentially a representation of total energy, namely heat (symbolized as fire, which is Shiva) and darkness (represented as black, which is Vishnu). We know that the limiting level of brightness is black. A simple example to realize this fact is that when one looks at the light liberated at the spot of arc welding, he or she realizes that looking at bright light results in blackout of vision.

A person may not realize that both light and darkness in their extreme limiting levels are the limiting maximum of energy or enthalpy, but scientists know this fact. Thus, the fact which is accepted by both science and religion (spiritualism) is that both brightness and darkness represent the state of limitless energy.

# 2  The Specialty of the Human Mind

## 2.1 Introduction

There are so many theories about the evolution of the world. But all these theories are based on the imagination and intuition of the authors, who conceived and narrated them. There are however many gaps in our knowledge, in both science and religion, when it comes to their quest to theorize about the formation and evolution of the world and its citizens. This was certainly true if we look at human history, there were many contradicting theories and a lot of confusion around the formation of the world, which in turn not only led to the birth of philosophical concepts like "nature", "God", and "supernatural power" but also kept them alive. We know that a large number of inventions and discoveries which were once just dreams or figments of imagination in the human mind have been realized. With the help of science, these dreams have blossomed into a number of scientific disciplines. Some of these inventions include the radio, television, motor car, aeroplane, rocket, satellites, etc. The main source of energy responsible for these wonderful inventions is the energy potential of the human mind.

But this kind of great ability is owned not just by the human mind alone. The very fact that many living species could be able to adjust to the environmental conditions of the surrounding in which they live, collect, and preserve their needs for their survival during periods of harsh environmental conditions reveals that they too have great cognitive power and spatial and temporal abilities. For instance, the rats living in farmlands mostly rely on the grains grown there. Indeed, food grains such as rice, wheat, corn, etc. are their main food source. But these foodgrains will be available only when they are fully grown and ready for harvest. This kind of situation will prevail only twice or thrice in a year, in the tropical zones, and maybe only once in a year in cold places, which are far above/below the equator. Therefore, the rats have to wait for long periods, between one harvest and the next, to get their food. To survive during the long period of a hard time, without any open food source, the rats living in such places cut a large number of ears of grain and stock them in their living tunnel holes for use during the period without food grains in the

DOI: 10.4324/9781003275527-2

farm field. In the same manner, squirrels, birds, etc. living in torrid zones, for their survival during the cold period when the ground is covered by a thick layer of snow, collect nuts containing the fat required for their living during this period of severe winter and store them in the holes in some selected tree trunks. They are able to judge which tree is suitable for making storage holes, and thus use them for their survival during the cold season.

Going beyond these examples, some creatures also do things which are possible only because they are highly intelligent and have the ability to learn. For example, gorillas break hard nuts with stones to eat the inner content. How do these monkeys know that only a material which is harder than the nut can break it open? Another example demonstrating intelligence among birds is the action of some crow species living in Japan. It can be said that these crows have thinking abilities similar to humans. They keep hard nuts, which cannot be broken with their beak, on main roads so that vehicles running on the roads can crush them. Also, they are intelligent enough to place the nuts in the middle of the road, where there is a traffic signal. When the nuts are crushed by the vehicles, the crows look for the red signal to glow so that traffic would stop. When the vehicles stop, the crows waiting there rush to the road and pick the eatable portions of the crushed nuts and fly away before traffic resumes. When we see these examples, it is natural to question the theory which states that the intellectual intuition is possible only for the human mind. Indeed, the mind-power of these animals and birds enables them to plan and execute ideas which call for intuitive thinking.

The human race has often expressed pride over the fact that they are intellectually superior to other creatures on Earth. The belief that "man is the measure of all things" is manifest in our institutions and works. However, many activities of the human race, which has certain arrogance about their mental capabilities and logical thinking, demonstrate their ignorance and bad judgement. Institutions set up by humankind, like the state and the government while grand in design are riddled in reality with many chinks which those with money and power are able to exploit freely and without consequence often at the expense of their fellow human beings. Society generally has not shown great intuition and judgement when faced with unfavourable or inconvenient choices. And we often see people chasing after unreason, superstition, and injustice.

## 2.2  Cause for This Confusion

The main cause or reason behind the confusion in realizing the power potential of the human mind is the mind itself. Early on, until the accident of railroad construction of foreman Phineas P. Gage (1823–1860), while doctors were discovering the features, functions, and make of human anatomy, including the eyes, ears, nose, and mouth among others, it was the human brain which was the most fascinating and mysterious. For a while, doctors and scientists were under the impression that the brain did not have an explicit purpose, which they could observe through experiments or observation. Indeed, the human brain was deemed as a less important organ since its importance was not yet discovered. In these early experiments by those studying human anatomy, the brain did not seem to have the ability to feel pain caused to it due to injuries, which was quite unusual. It was only after the medical science branch neurology was born, the medical world realized that the pains such as carbuncle, heart disease, cough, sore eye, cold, sprain, headache, whitlow, piles, and fever encountered by any part of our body were realized by us because the brain senses these pains. We know that before performing any surgery, physicians give anaesthesia to make the patient unconscious. In this state, the brain is made to sleep so that it will make the body not to feel the pain caused by the surgery.

If some of the nerves in the brain lobe are cut, say by a knife, the person will not feel any pain, in accordance with the findings of the medical science that the brain nerves are not equipped with sensing the pain caused to itself. Because of this peculiar nature of the brain, scientists were under the impression that the brain is the only useless part of the human body until the following miracle happened. The following anecdote is quite popularly known as the event that allowed doctors to discover the function of the human brain and observe its peculiarities and mysteries which we are still discovering today many decades later. In 1848, a 25-year-old railroad worker named Phineas Gage while working on a railway line, blowing up rocks to clear the way in Cavendish, VT, got hurt. His job was to drill a hole, place an explosive charge in it, and pack it with sand using a 13-pound metal bar known as a tamping iron.

He got injured when the metal bar created a spark that touched off the charge which drove the "tamping iron up and out of the hole, through his left cheek, behind his eye socket, and out of the top of his head" (Harlow, 2017).

Gage survived but the injury caused irreparable damage to his brain's left frontal lobe. It was reported that Gage's personality changed completely after his injury.

"He is fitful, irreverent, indulging at times in the grossest profanity, which was not previously his custom", John Martyn Harlow, the physician who treated Gage after the accident, reported this.

According to Malcolm Macmillan, an honorary professor at the Melbourne School of Psychological Sciences and the author of *An Odd Kind of Fame: Stories of Phineas Gage*, this sudden personality transformation caused Gage to show up in all medical textbooks.

"He was the first case where you could say fairly definitely that injury to the brain produced some kind of change in personality", according to Macmillan.

And that was a big deal in the mid-1800s, when the brain's purpose and inner workings were largely a mystery. At the time, phrenologists were still assessing people's personalities by measuring bumps on their skull.

"Gage's famous case would help establish brain science as a field", according to Allan Ropper, a neurologist at Harvard Medical School and Brigham and Women's Hospital.

Dr. John Harlow, who treated Gage following the accident, noted his personality change in an 1851 edition of the *American Phrenological Journal and Repository of Science* (NPR, 2017).

## 2.3  Brain, the God or Nature

The case of Phineas Gage became quite famous, the story is often repeated in scientific circles as the event or moment when doctors discovered the importance of the brain. The story showcases the fascination that humans have always had with curious medical cases involving the brain.

Many doctors and neurologists studied Gage's brain to understand the personality change and the injury. The team of doctors, after getting the approval of a judge, opened Gage's skull and observed his brain. To their surprise, the hole in the brain nerves system, made by the crowbar had disappeared. Their study revealed that the hole which parted the brain into two portions gradually narrowed and finally the two parts in his brain healed together. Was this an act of God, nature, or a result of something that occurred in the human brain?

The observations and inferences by the doctors not only made them curious about the anatomy of the human brain but also made them consider the possibility that the brain affects human thought and action. This sad event made the medical world reconsider their assumptions about the brain. This resulted in the birth of one of the involved disciplines in medical science, namely neurology. Ever since then, many neurologists have gone back to study Gage's case again since this was a case which started the field of neurology.

Even though the brain cannot feel the pain caused by any damage to itself, it is the main controller of the human body system, including the thought process and intuition. The thinking and intuitive power of the brain is dictated by the arrangement of its nerves, which are stacked in different layers. The medical world began the research to get an insight into the link between the nerve system and brainpower. Thus, though cruel, the killing of the popular surgeon by the prisoner paved the way for the emerging of a new branch of medical science, which strives hard to understand the human brain. The beauty of this science is that it gets the wisdom for its research from the object which it is trying to analyse.

## 2.4  What Is Intelligence?

The question of human intelligence is a complex one, there are many tests which are designed to measure it. But if we were to simplify this question and make judgements only on the basis of human action, I would categorize them into two groups. One group is that who do whatever they do, simply because others do them; these are people with herd mentality, and the basis of this action can be many but in the context of the potential of the mind, I would infer that this is often a result of ignorance. The second group is that who analyse and judge whatever they do. This mind has the power to look at the reasons for performing an act, analyse the consequences, and then decide whether what they do is worth doing.

The experience we gain from our encounters we face in the world is often a better education than what we acquire in schools. The education and knowledge we get from our practical experiences often have a more lasting impression on us and are more powerful. Education is a tool which we use to gain knowledge of things near and far away. It essentially removes the ignorance covering the wisdom of the mind. Wisdom therefore is not alien to our minds but an essential part of it which our experiences and education help nurture. You could say that we are born with a layer covering the wisdom in our minds. Education helps us remove the cover and tap into it. Swami Vivekananda quite fittingly said, "Education is the manifestation of the perfection already in man" (Gosling, 2007).

From the life of great scholars, we can learn that they did not have the feeling that they were highly qualified. In fact, many of them were aware that what they had encashed as invention or discovery was just a negligible fraction of the limitless brainpower.

People who follow along with others without thinking about their reasons for doing so are not in tune with their minds, they may even not have clear knowledge about their likes and dislikes. A person who is cut off from their own mind and who do not deeply think about or analyse the reasoning or the implications of their actions do not have their own set of moral principles. Their morals, sense of right and wrong, and their justifications for actions are merely based on learned responses which they adopt from their surroundings, or school which do have roots that are flimsy and can change easily, with or without reasons.

The lack of self-reflection leads to a life lived without moral scruples. While our circumstances do determine the kind of life we lead, our choices and actions are heavily dependent on our influences and the degrees of self-reflection—reflecting on our actions and how they affect others. We do see people who live their everyday life with great dignity and sincerity—towards themselves, their neighbours, and strangers. People who use the rational power of their minds to reason, question, and act according to their own principles and values can never justify acting in a way which is unconscionable, which will corrupt or go against reason, and their sense of right and wrong.

The power of intellectual mind is very high, and it is very difficult to spoil the logical intuitive power of such a mind. I always wonder how people believe in astrology—the earth revolves around the sun in an elliptical path, in addition to spinning about its own axis. The moon is a satellite moving around the earth. The moon shines because of the sunlight falling on it. Mars, Venus, Uranus, Neptune, Pluto, and Saturn are some of the planets among the infinite number of planets in the vast celestial space. In its moving path, when moon comes between the sun and the earth, the shadow of the moon falls on earth. Similarly, when the earth comes between the sun and the moon, the shadow of earth falls on the moon. These are called astronomical events for science, but the astrology calls these as eclipse.

Some people with the intention of exploiting the ignorance of innocent people on the pretext of astrology and make them believe that these astrological events have powerful influence on the day-to-day life of humans, and thus make a comfortable living by charging for their predictions. If your mind treats the stars and planets as astronomical objects and their movements are governed by astronomical rules such as Kepler's law, then you might not believe that the movement of a planet could cause you to lose your job. Is astrology a practice of escapism practised by many? Here it is essential for us to realize the fact that the energy of the sun is limitless, and the enormous amount of energy emitted by the sun is responsible for the evolution and growth of all living species on our earth. The huge quantum of energy contained in its light is the potential of sun. This energy potential exists in the form of heat. Because of this, sciences such as thermodynamics (Zemanskey, 1968), heat transfer (Rathakrishnan, 2012), and quantum mechanics (Rathakrishnan, 2015; Griffiths and Schroeter, 2018) treat the energy or enthalpy as thermal energy. May be the practice of calling something as good and pleasant as *warmth* came from the realization that the heat energy given by the sun is the main source of energy required for the life of all the species on earth.

## 2.5 Greatness of Intuitive Mind

Intelligent minds equipped with intuition and reasoning will decide and accept something only after analysing the consequences that might result from the events taking place. They are not likely to believe and accept something simply because they see others doing it. Such people are able to hone their cognitive abilities well since they are constantly challenging their thinking capabilities. Great scientists who contributed greatly to society through their inventions and discoveries were people with great intuition and reasoning, they were observant and challenged themselves and others around them. A typical example of this is the scientist Thomas Alva Edison (1847–1931).

Edison was quite special in many respects, including in his potential to work in both theoretical and applied sciences. Starting from the electrical bulb, Edison invented many hundreds of new things, which helped the world to live in comfort. No other scientist had developed so many new things which we use in our daily lives as Edison did. He experienced many ups and downs in his career and faced many hardships, although he was never swayed. He is a perfect example of someone not letting their failures discourage them.

A powerful mind remains stable, and does not lose its balance even when it encounters limitless wealth and fame. If a person is blessed with a high level of intellectual potential yearning for power, wealth, and fame, I would not hold the person in high regard. Great minds do not easily get cowed even under extraordinary circumstances. Edison treated many great events in his life as ordinary and kept moving ahead making new inventions and discoveries. When he did not succeed in his attempt to make the electric bulb after innumerable tries, he did not let this hamper his interest. With his persistence and hard work, he was finally successful in making the electric bulb. The entire world celebrated this great achievement. According to a famous anecdote, a group of press reporters interviewed Professor Edison and one of them asked him what made him continue working after failing for so many times. He supposedly remarked that he never failed, he instead proved that those failed 940 experiments were simply not how to make a blub, if you try any of those you will be unsuccessful.

Edison not only had a great mind but he also was never swayed by fame. A fair and balanced attitude towards failure and disappointment is fairly hard to achieve. It is possible only for those who work for the sake of solving problems and creating new things and not because it brings them wealth or glory. A stable mind is even-keeled and treats everything as equal, whether it is gold or mud. You might say that it is quite similar to the mind of the child which has not been socially conditioned yet. Before they are conditioned to behave in certain set ways, children are not fazed when they fail to achieve something or finish a task, they do not get dejected with failures. For example, while learning to walk, it is quite common for children to fall down repeatedly. But in spite of these repeated failures to balance their weight on their feet and walk, the child will attempt to get up continuously until they learn to walk steadily. This attitude is a gift from nature. Further, during childhood, they do not have any strong or set likes or dislikes. Their likes and dislikes are based on their whims or their immediate thoughts and wants. This kind of well-balanced mental state prevails until a child enters into their teenage years. When a child enters this stage, the outside world starts affecting their lives and internal thoughts considerably. They are quite suddenly very much affected by how they are perceived by those around them. Their mind transitions and their thoughts, emotions, and actions are less uninhibited as they learn more about themselves and about social mores and conventions. While these social and cognitive changes are quite natural, it is easy for both young adolescents and adults to let the outside world have control over their thoughts and behaviours.

Feelings of desire, wants, conceit, and greed are like a perturbation, it is not bad in small doses. It becomes dangerous only when it grows to a considerable level. When it is within the limit of ambition, it will not make one lose his balance; but when it goes beyond, the person whether young or old will most likely trip and fall. The levels of these emotions which will force a person to lose their equilibrium is not fixed, it varies from person to person. This is the law of nature.

We often use the word "urge" to connotate negative emotions—for desires which grow without limit, for example, the desire to amass wealth without effort, the desire to occupy high power, the desire to earn great fame which that person does not deserve. But if the mind has the urge to work for whatever it aims at acquiring and the urge listens to that advice, then the person can work hard to achieve the goals he/she desires to achieve (Premji, 2022). Gandhi's writings show how he engaged with problems deeply. His actions were thought out based on his philosophies of non-violence, truth, and self-reliance. Everything he did had a motive, he believed that offering service to mankind was like offering service to God. He also believed that education should focus on physical, intellectual, and spiritual development of young minds for them to grow into responsible, intelligent, and kind people.

The following is a quote from the great book in Tamil literature (Thiruvalluvar, 1986):

> Even those who scaled the mountain of morality will not be able to hold their anger even for a second.
>
> (Verse 29)

The essence of this verse is that controlling negative emotions like anger is very hard even for a person who is upstanding and has an impeccable moral and ethical record. No human can win over anger in the entire universe. This fact is true even for great saints who according to the legend practised the art of not letting any emotions control them. Greediness, anger, and deceit are some of the heavy, unwanted loads we make the mind to shoulder. Many people struggle and suffer due to their inability to shoulder these loads. But it is important to practice the art of controlling extreme emotions, setting aside these evil loads to travel smoothly with pleasure and peace of mind on your life path.

The free time a mind gets has a dominant role in making the mind waver. The mind of one who gets himself involved in something which he likes never gets tired. The main reason for this is that the mind which is engaged in something fascinating to it, such as science for a scientist and music for a musician, does not have time to think of the body in which it is living. Because of this, the body having such a great mind is energetic all the time.

## 2.6 Youth and Old Age

For every living species, the mind and body act together. In this journey, the one which is in the driver's seat is the mind. This is common to all species, beginning from the plant kingdom to humans. In this situation, there is a possible danger of the sixth sense or the intuitive thinking to become an enemy to the person. This might be somewhat confusing to us. Let us look at the following examples from nature which might help us understand this theory a little better.

The four stages—the birth, growth, ageing, and end—are common to all living things. But the periods or duration of these stages differ, sometimes even extraordinarily, from species to species. In the plant kingdom, the banyan tree can live up to as long as 700 years. In contrast to this, the trees which have a very short life span of only a few years are the drumstick or horseradish tree and *Sesbania grandiflora* tree. From the day the seed germinates, a banyan plant will take about 10–15 years to appear like a tree. But a drumstick plant will become a tree in about six months from the day its seed germinates. Therefore, it may be stated with confidence that anything which grows slow and steady will live long and which has rapid growth is short-lived. Let us look at two animals to gain further insight into this law of nature. An elephant can live for 100 years. But animals like lion and tiger have an average life span of about ten years only. There is enough scope to conclude that the life span of a species has a direct relation to its gestation period. An elephant calf grows in the mother's womb for 22 months, whereas babies of lion and tiger gain full shape within about 60 days of entering the mother's womb. These examples validate the thought that things which grow slowly have longer lifespan than those which grow fast.

This implies that there is a direct relationship between growth rate and lifespan. If we keep this inference in mind, we may understand the human mind to some extent. If a person want their mind to acquire more power or become more agile, they should not expect quick results; instead, they should work towards the goal without any expectations. Indeed, it should have the tendency to ignore the modest benefit which might surface during its travel to the goal of very high power, until it reaches the goal. For example, let us assume that one wishes to become a scientist of a high calibre so that they can find a place in history. They would have to work hard to achieve this goal from a young age, not necessarily towards becoming a scientist but towards honing their reasoning and thinking skills. Having a good and stimulating environment is also very essential for them to achieve their goal. This kind of environment and experience will stimulate the power potential of the mind all the time. This stimulation would ensure that the mind is active and productive and the person's actions will reflect their confidence in the thoughts and choices they make.

# 3 Views of Theism and Atheism

## 3.1 Introduction

It is almost unanimously believed that there is some power which is beyond the perception of the human mind. This great power is responsible for the movements of the universe. This hypothesis is accepted by both theists and atheists, without any dispute. But the interpretation given by these two groups to this great power is subject to great dispute. The power which could neither be understood nor be explained was given the name *God* by theists and many gave it the name "nature".[1] There are many different sects and beliefs in this world. The world of theism and atheism quarrels about the existence of God and other spiritual entities, but most sects do have devised some ways of explaining the existence of power in the universe which gives life and energy to all.

Now, let us think about our stand on this great power, which controls the universe. Irrespective of the name or symbolic representation given to it, the faith about the existence of some great power itself is enough for inducing self-reliance and confidence to a common man. One of the oldest sects of human race, namely the Tamils, keep thinking about this great power, which is the source of energy; questions and debates about this is seen in many ancient literary and philosophical works in Tamil. The outcome of this long research resulted in the famous quote: "Those realized this power did not narrate it and those narrated it did not realise it" (Thirumoolar, 1994). The statement implies that there were people who were debating and thinking about the existence of this ultimate power which was the source of all energy and creation. According to this quote, this power can only be felt and cannot be explained or described. This description also fits with the description of intelligence or wisdom. As we know, wisdom of a person can only be inferred from his deeds and cannot be seen physically.

When we look at ancient philosophical and spiritual texts, we see the presence of both belief and doubt. This is evidence of the human preoccupation with unravelling the mysteries of the universe and their own minds. These kinds of questions paved the way for many scientific inventions of great value. Can we say without any doubt that only the human mind is capable of rational

DOI: 10.4324/9781003275527-3

thinking or possesses intuition after observing nature and other creatures? We cannot. Observations like this have revealed that thinking power is there in the minds of all living species. There is enough evidence to support this thought. But the important inference from this discussion is that so far no one has understood all the elements or the complete potential of the nature of the universe or the great controller of the living world, namely the mind.

*Atheism* is the belief that there is no Supreme Being or deity. In other words, *atheism* is the denial of the existence of God or of any gods. In everyday life, many people define natural phenomena without the need of a god or gods. They do not deny the existence of one or more gods; they simply say that this existence is not necessary. Gods do not provide a purpose to life, nor influence it, according to this view. Many scientists practice what they call methodological naturalism. They silently adopt philosophical naturalism and use the scientific method. Their belief in a god does not affect their results. Agnostics say that it cannot be known if a god or gods exist. In their view, strong atheism requires a leap of faith.

Practical atheism can take different forms: (1) Absence of religious motivation—belief in gods does not motivate moral action, religious action, or any other form of action. (2) Active exclusion of the problem of gods and religion from intellectual pursuit and practical action. (3) Indifference—the absence of any interest in the problems of gods and religion. (4) Unawareness of the concept of a deity.

## 3.2  Ways to Stimulate Mind Power

The facts we analysed about the human mind so far raise a basic doubt about the possibility of liberating the enormous potential that is contained within the mind (Rathakrishnan, 2021). If it is possible, what are the ways to do so? Let us look into this important aspect and read more about the ways someone could tap into the energy of their mind or intellectual capability. If we are mindful of our surroundings and nature, it will be of immense help to this investigation. Ancient philosophers and seers spent a lot of time on ruminating on the mysteries of the mind and their surroundings.

In ancient texts, there are stories of saints and ascetics who learnt how to perfectly control their mind and thereby acquired some mystic powers. These mystic powers symbolize the limitless power of the human mind. What are the things which stimulate the minds of great artists, poets, and philosophers? The following examples will help us look at natural events to understand the power of mind and the ways to bring that for application. Usually during summer, when the sky is clear, we can enjoy the magnificent beauty of the full moon. Many of us have this experience. If the full moon is viewed in the lake water, pond, or river, we hear that this scenery liberates the aesthetic potential of poets and artists. For a common man also, this kind of beautiful scenery gives immense pleasure. But to view the beauty of a full moon, travelling in space, in a pond or tank, the water has to be still, without any disturbance such as turbulent waves, and free of contamination such as polluting chemicals and so on, which might spoil the transparency of water. If there is any perturbation in the water, we will not be able to enjoy the beauty of the full moon in that water. In other words, to enjoy the beauty of the shining moon in water, the water has to be clear and free of any disturbance. This implies that any reflection will be clear only when the reflecting media is free of perturbation. This experience implies that the image shown by a clear medium is beautiful. This kind of calmness, without any disturbances, is the first step to tap into the potential of the mind. This kind of power can be attained by a mind which is free of any disturbance because "nothing will go wrong for a calm mind".

Let us see the scientific reason for this. When a person becomes angry, emotional, or stressed, it causes a biological response, their body warms up, the circulation of blood speeds up, and their heart pumps faster. Because of the faster pumping, even though the volume of the blood circulated is larger, the emotional state makes the blood to circulate at a higher speed to all parts of the body and adversely affects the blood supply to the brain. Thus, turbulent emotions like fear, anger, greediness, etc. reduce the blood flow to the brain nerves. Extreme and prolonged emotional reactions and stress disrupts the process that regulates blood flow and wreaks havoc on the natural balance in many regions of the brain. A person who cannot learn how to control and overcome extreme emotional reactions or gets easily swayed by external circumstances cannot learn how to efficiently use the potential or power of their minds and over time their minds are dulled or silenced.

Learning to master extreme emotions and stress and keeping your mind calm and peaceful always comes with practice and discipline. Our minds are usually calm while we are asleep, the heart pumps at a normal rate, and the brain is alert and active. But is it possible for people to calm the mind while awake?

While keeping the body in an inactive state, it is possible to focus the mind on something which is pleasing. Theoretically, while in this state, blood circulation to different parts of the body (which is without any movement) will be reduced, and a higher rate of blood will circulate to the brain, which is active. This increased circulation will activate the brain nerves system, resulting in the emission of powerful waves. Neurons and glial cells regulate blood flow in the brain. A thorough understanding of the activates of these cells is the key for understanding the brain activity. This is the focus of science of neurology (Greene and Bone, 2007).

I believe that many of the great names in history may have practised some version of this technique of centring yourself. This practice stimulates the power potential of the mind, and uses the energy when required.

If we observe or read the works or the life accounts of scientists, great poets or saints, you will find in them both a calm focus which I believe made them tap into mysterious recesses of their minds which allow them to use the full potential of their intellectual capabilities and create wonderful inventions.

While discussing the lives of scientists and poets like these, one cannot help but wonder if these great minds after achieving what they did not give in to greater ambitions, or greed. I believe that it is our intuitive power which regulates our emotions, and helps keep the mind balanced. Because of rational thinking, the mind can allow one to enjoy pleasures in a disciplined manner.

Mind power is the basis for both science and spiritualism. When we practise to liberate the power of our mind, there is a possibility that that person's mind could get agitated. Thinking calmly and rationally when faced with emotionally turbulent situations and controlling stress and extreme emotions are quite important for the mind power to be liberated. Persons who followed this practice are able to achieve great success and tranquillity. People like the Buddha and Newton and Einstein are examples of this. It should be noted that the keen observation on the events taking place in the process of reaching the result they want to archive and the single-minded devotion to their work till reaching the goal is regarded as meditation here.

There are theories which suggest that extreme environments and adverse conditions teach people to deal with stressful situations early in life, and they develop coping mechanism to overcome their environment. We see an example of this in countries which are more prone to natural disasters: the development of earthquake proof buildings constructed by the Japanese, and heating and cooling systems developed by the Europeans to protect them from harsh winter and summer are some examples for the developments due to the environmental fury. Similarly, the period during the two world wars was a time when many inventions of missiles, fighter planes, machine guns, etc. were made, which then led to other inventions and discoveries, speeding up the clock of scientific discovery.

Now our mind may ask the following questions which are more fundamental in nature. Is it possible to raise or increase the power potential of a mind or tap into it more directly, especially in moments and situations where one might feel are their lowest? The answer to this question is a definite *yes*. Yes, it is possible to stimulate your mind or to practice making your mind calmer and release its potential to a greater extent. But to arouse a mind which is indolent and cannot overcome problems or stressful situations involves great effort. This requires us to follow the laws of motion, according to Newton's first law of motion, "to change a system from its inertial state an external force should act on it". To wake up the nerves of a mind when in rest or asleep due to either laziness or fear and anxiety requires a lot of effort. And after the mind is awake, it further needs to be trained to bring out its true potential. Continued training and practice can liberate the energy potential of the mind to a great extent similar to the training musicians undergo to gain the power required to remember and reproduce thousands tunes and their variations. Let us have a closer look at the exercise of musicians.

## 3.3 Clarity of Music

It is well known that all forms of music are the outcome of the sound notes; sa, re, ga, ma, pa, dha, ni in the Hindustani and Carnatic musical traditions. Different combinations of these nodes and their sonnets stretching result in different tunes. But by the mathematical permutation and combination of these seven sound nodes, we get a total of 170,012 tunes. The tunes of various styles of music of different countries of the world are confined to these 170,012 tunes. Now it is easy to realize that no one in the world can master even the names of these many tunes prevailing in the music. This information about music clearly demonstrates that it is impossible to measure and quantify the potential of mind which has these many, humanly unmanageable music tunes as just a module of its power potential. In other words, it may be stated that like the unmanageable quantum of musical tunes, the potential of the mind is also immeasurable. The very fact that in spite of the continued efforts by scientists and philosophers, the power potential of the mind is yet to be understood is the testimony for the quantum of the power embedded in the mind.

## 3.4 What Is the Way to Measure It?

Something which cannot be quantified precisely is referred to as mathematics. Speaking in mathematical terms, we can say that the potential of the mind is infinitely large. The attempt to measure and understand the magnitude of this infinite potential of mind with the help of mind itself may be called philosophy. People attempting to understand the power potential of the mind and regulate it to use for philanthropic service, by following a particular philosophical path, are called "Siddhars" in the Tamil world.[2] Among the Siddhars, the saint named Thirumoolar is quite famous, he is said to have had great control over his mind and knowledge about the mind far beyond what we generally know. He composed 3,000 verses in the book *Thirumandhiram* (Thirumoolar, 1994) narrating the power of mind, ways to liberate its energy, and its use for a noble cause. "Mandhiram" in Tamil means the potential of the mind. In this book, saint Thirumoolar lays down the numerous ways in which the immense energy within a person's mind can be liberated and channelled for service.

In essence, *Thirumandhiram* says that if someone trains his mind systematically, it is possible to liberate the immense energy it has, and use that energy for surprising feats of bravery and intelligence, which may not be possible for a common person.

A veritable personification of these methods discussed by Thirumoolar to arouse the mind is Saint Ramalinga Swamigal (October 5, 1823 to January 30, 1874), who lived in Tamil Nadu, India. According to the British Gazette

(Francis, 2022), Saint Ramalinga Swamigal is reported to have transformed his body into light, by intense spiritual practice.

In the perspective of the author, these stories of incredible and miraculous feats by mere humans is present in many cultures; these are shared as stories and myths of superhuman figures who were able to learn more about the mysteries of the mind and the universe which we cannot see and learn because our minds are not capable of absorbing information of this order. A lot of compelling accounts exist and are repeated because we are curious to know more about the unknown. Our minds want to be challenged and we want to both preserve and gain more knowledge of everything which remains undiscovered.

Attaining samadhi or the great silence is the end goal for many schools of spirituality in India. In many written accounts about the saints and in mythology, we find descriptions of saints and ascetics who trained from a young age to mediate give up worldly desires and possessions to live a life of penury and work only towards seeking knowledge by looking within. Many of these sadhus learned to control their mind and liberate its energy potential. Meditation removes all the perturbations in the mind and enables it to concentrate on one single thought. A single-minded prolonged practice of meditation must bring immense peace and calm to the mind. According to these accounts of saints and sages of old, many also say that when these ascetics or saints (like Thirumoolar [Thirumoolar, 1994] and Arunagirinathar [Thiruppugaz, 1986]) attained this great silence, they were rendered speechless.

There are many schools and businesses around the world which advertise that they train people on how to meditate and improve their lives. These schools and retreats charge exorbitant fees to train people in meditation and educate them about the mind and spirituality. They offer easy and quick exercises and/or literature to tap into the potential of their minds and bodies. Their advertisements often make claims that they have experts who are trained in meditation and many of these people are often treated like sadhus or spiritual guides by people.

The lives of sadhus like Thirumoolar, and Arunagirinathar are quite different from those of the modern spiritual guide or sadhus. While it is true that the world has changed very rapidly in recent history, the basic teachings and practices of schools which ascetics and sadhus join have remained the same, at least in principle. It takes great discipline and focus to practice meditation. The lives of these well-known ascetics is a life of hardship and penury which they chose deliberately so that they could exercise their mind, gain control of their minds and emotions to gain truth and knowledge.

It is essential to know the difference between practising spirituality as career on which you rely on for money and other material wants and desires and living a spiritual life in which the purpose of living the life of a mendicant is to bring great discipline in order to solely focus on knowing more about the mind and the world.

Is there a way then to measure and quantify the power potential of mind? Are there any means to do that or will this question never be answered? We are going to venture into the project of finding a convincing answer for this involved, confused, and complex state.

The formation of the nerves system in the mind is responsible for both abstract or theoretical and applied thinking power of the mind.

Abstract thinking allows the mind to think conceptually, put things in perspective, and reason them out. This allows those who excel in abstract thinking to create scientific inventions and discoveries. Applied thinking allows people to effectively implement these concepts. While many great scientists were (are) blessed with theoretical thinking, only very few are blessed with the combination of abstract and applied thinking power (Murphy, 2001). This kind of mind equipped with both the powers is capable of doing miraculously great things. I believe the mind of Thomas Alva Edison is a typical example for this. We have briefly discussed Edison's life and scientific career. It was due to his great ability to think abstractly which allowed him to conceive his inventions and because he possessed applied thinking ability, he was able to carry out this experiment in an organized way and to swap out old ideas with new ones to test out.

Another great scientists blessed with mind capable of theoretical thinking of a very high calibre was Albert Einstein. I believe that while Oppenheimer possessed a very high level of applied thinking power (Rouze and Oppenheimer, 2023), Einstein invented the energy identity and Oppenheimer used this relation to develop the atomic bomb.

Other examples of minds possessing both theoretical and applied thinking are Thomas Alva Edison and G.D. Naidu, a renowned scientist (Biography, 2013). Both of them were able to grasp abstract concepts of physics very easily. G.D. Naidu lived in India (March 23, 1893 to January 4, 1974). The scientific achievements of Naidu seem astonishing even to the scientific world. The plantain tree which would yield only once was made to yield twice by Naidu.

Naidu studied only up to middle school. He was forced to discontinue school education because of family circumstances and he instead got a job as a helper in an automobile repair shop. Within a few months of joining, Naidu was able to grasp and understand the functioning of the different parts of automobile engines.

One day, on the street of the workshop where Naidu worked, a British Government official came on a Royal Enfield motorcycle. Exactly in front of the workshop, the motorcycle stopped working. The officer could not understand why it had stopped. He tried to start it repeatedly, but the motorcycle did not start. He came to the workshop and asked them to attend to his motorcycle. A senior technician of the workshop came to attend to the problem. The technician tried his best but the motorcycle would not work. The officer realized that his motorcycle will not function immediately and decided to leave.

At that time, the little boy Naidu decided to offer his help and asked if he could try his hand at making the motorcycle work. The British officer allowed him. Naidu as a small boy observed its parts keenly and after making some adjustments requested the officer to start the motorbike. In just one kick the motorcycle started. Other mechanics watching were quite startled. The officer was pleasantly surprised and offered some money to Naidu that he refused. Instead, he asked the officer if he would permit Naidu to dismantle and then assemble his motorcycle. The officer was surprised with the curiosity of the boy and permitted him to do so. The next day, in front of the public gathered there, Naidu quickly dismantled the motorcycle part-by-part and with the same agility assembled it back, having never done it before or have even seen most of the parts.

The desire, enthusiasm, and sharpness of Naidu impressed the officer. He thanked the boy profusely. This level of curiosity remained in his mind throughout his life.

Naidu's mind would not have scaled to the levels it later did had he accepted the money offered by the British man. The urge to learn more only grew stronger in Naidu in later life.

The efforts of saints and scientists who tried to understand the brain are quite fascinating to read. Our minds have unbounded, limitless energy potential, but we are yet to get clear insights into the formation, strength, and weakness of the brain. Philosophically, we may think that the reason for this is that nature does not want us to have a thorough understanding of mind since it might lead humans to create inventions of mass destruction and eradicate all life on earth.

### 3.5  Concept of God

Since the conception of human life, the question about the existence of God has continuously confused humanity and has caused them to go to extreme lengths to seek answers, including going on pilgrimages, fasting, waging wars, writing treatises, building opulent temples and churches in God's name, among other things. But there has also always been factions which believe and those who are non-believers. The clash between religious sects or those who believe and those who are opposed to them is quite ubiquitous in the history of civilization. However, there are certain questions about the existence, energy, or power of the mind which are unanswered, this fact is accepted by many of these factions. Those who do not believe in the concept of God refer to this power as nature, for example, the Buddhist sect Shinto believes that the sun, wind, space, fire, ocean, etc. are responsible for the life on earth and worship these natural things as "light". Indeed, in Shinto Shrines, there is no practice of idol worship, they worship the nature in the form of light.

Before moving further, we should get a glimpse into other views on God and practices of worship.

People of the Jewish faith believe that there is a single God who not only created the universe, but with whom every Jewish person can also have an individual and personal relationship. They believe that God continues to work in the world, affecting everything that people do. The Jewish relationship with God is a covenant.

There is no concept of God in Buddhism. Buddhism is about how *you* relate to *yourself*, and focuses on learning how we operate internally, so that we can stop reacting with unhappiness and instead learn to become happy. No outside power can do this for us, so God has no role in Buddhism. Buddhism is perhaps the first workable style of psychological growth.

In Christianity, God is the eternal being who created the universe and all there is. God is usually held to have the properties of holiness, justice, omnipotence, omniscience, omnibenevolence, omnipresence, and immortality.

Jains do not believe in a God or gods in the way that many other religions do, but they do believe in divine (or at least perfect) beings that are worthy of devotion.

Islamic doctrine emphasizes the oneness, uniqueness, transcendence, and utter otherness of God. As such, God is different from anything that the human senses can perceive or that the human mind can imagine. The God of Islam encompasses all creation, but no mind can fully encompass or grasp him. In *Sikhism, God* is conceived as the Oneness that permeates the entirety of creation and beyond.

Though the religions appear to differ in their practices, the nuclei or prime principle about which all revolve is that "there exists a power which governs the evolution of the universe". Some religion terms this as *God* and some other term this power as nature. A we saw, the faith which realizes the supreme power as god is "theism" and the one which refers the power as nature is "atheism".

As a disciple of Bernard Shaw, who has keenly observed the tussle between the groups on the concept or hypothesis of God, I believe (Rathakrishnan, 2021) that God is a hypothetical concept proposed by a few to regulate humanity. Therefore, we are forced to take the stand that both the stances— "there exists God" and "there is no God"— are correct. The justification for our stand is quite confusing and similar to the fact that we are seeking wisdom to understand the power of our own mind.

Anyone who analyses faith and religious philosophy without any bias would say that the arguments and faith of both theists and atheists are correct. Indeed, when my mind attempts to analyse and understand the hypotheses of God and nature which try to accommodate the boundless power of mind within these nomenclature has a confusion of an order more than yours. But silence has to prevail after a cyclone. Therefore, presuming that the thorough confusion, perturbation, and turbulence dominate our mind when venturing into the analysis of mind power, we will eventually have some understanding about the problem we have at hand.

## 3.6 Benefits of Theism

The main objective of theism is to induce confidence in the mind. A person with confidence can only be victorious in all his ventures. A person walking alone in a dark night will walk without fear if he believes that the grace of the almighty is with him. This kind of faith will make the person reach his destination comfortably. Thus, the faith that God's grace is with him makes him reach the goal. This simple example enables us to get an impression of the power of theism. The power of spiritualism is to give this kind of benefit. Now another doubt might come to our mind: if the person walking in the darkness is a brave person, where is the need for the faith in God for his journey. For this kind of mind with self-confidence, there is no need of theism. Indeed, this kind of people with extremely high level of confidence also becomes speechless. But, in the group with high self-confidence also, there are many fake characters. These people, in order to show that their mind power is high, might scold and criticize the theist. Thus, there are fake persons among both theists and atheists.

Another important advantage of theism is that it nurtures socialism and unity of society. During the festive time, affluent people provide water, eatables, and sometimes meal too to the devotees coming to the places of worship. If we just think about the inner sense in this deed, we can easily discern the social service hidden in this act. Theism is a doctrine proposed to result in this kind of noble deeds, mostly essential for social amenity. But scientific evolution, globalization, and half-baked knowledge due to substandard education gave a jolt and shook the very foundation of theism.

In ancient days, humans were afraid of the natural events such as thunder, lightning, cyclone, tsunami, earthquake, and volcanic eruption. Because of the fear, people began to worship these powers of nature, with the faith that the prayer will safeguard them from these furies. This prayer led to the worship of the five basic elements constituting the universe. Further, humans also realized that their body is made up of these five elements. Some real sages who realized this truth came down from their speechless state and with the aim of directing humanity to a peaceful and happy life symbolized fire as Lord Shiva, rain as Lord Indra, wind as Lord Vayu, etc.

The medical science today is clear about the need for the balance of the five basic elements: the muscle (land), blood (water), breath (air), temperature (heat), and space (the space in the ear) in a body must be in proper balance for health. Even if one of these is out of balance, the person will fall sick. Another important feature is if one of these ceases to exist, the person will not be alive.

The sages who were aware of these facts, even in ancient times when medical science did not evolve, revealed these facts in a philosophical manner. One such philosophical verse is the following one sung by saint Thayumanava Swamigal (Natarajan, 1978):

The life made up of the five basic elements is like an air-bubble in water.

Theism is a doctrine proposed to induce confidence in the mind of a common man who does not have any idea about the facts revealed by sages or present-day medical science. We can notice that during festive days, the deities taken out in procession take shape depending on the artists who make and decorate them and all these symbolic shapes are patronized by the public. Thus, it may be inferred that the idols of God we see in the places of worship are not those worshipped in the ancient days. But for the common folk, rituals and traditions which their immediate ancestors followed or their community follows are important and sacred since it gives them a sense of identity and belonging. Rituals and processions which are carried out with much pomp do not bring any spiritual or emotional peace or comfort, they are however the only visible forms of religious practice.

This does not mean that I am preaching atheism. It is however important to discuss the trappings which religious practices have become bogged down in and the hypocritical practices which organized religion partakes in. The saint who wrote *Bhagavad Gita* had said, "Action is thy duty, not the fruity". This means do your duty wholeheartedly and the rewards for you efforts will come to you. This message is conveyed in *Krishna Kaviam* (Rathakrishnan, 2021) as follows:

> If the profession for this birth decided by the almighty is performed with single minded devotion with a great status, which will make even the heaven become yours and you will rise high and rule the world.

The philosophy of theism has value and it holds an immense power over its followers. But at present, many people without realizing the meaning of such a powerful doctrine surrender to those who would rather lead them astray for their personal gain.

## 3.7  Essence of Theism

Theism or the belief in God is a philosophical practice in many religions to regulate the mind to proceed on the suitable path. For a merchant, theism will direct him to live in balance like a scale.

For a teacher, theism will direct his conscience to indulge fully, immerse completely in teaching and research, and work with a single-minded devotion. Like this, theism will devise schemes to people of different profession in different stages of their lives.

It will direct a mind with inclination towards life of asceticism to follow and attain sainthood. A suitable example for this kind of mind is the life of saint Pattinathaar. Pattinathaar was a businessman who lived in Kaveripoom-pattinam in Tanjore district of Tamil Nadu in the 10th century. He was so rich that he was able to extend the loan of a large sum of money to the Chola King of his time. His name was Thiruvenkadar. One day he saw a note which said, "even an eyeless needle will not come with you at the end". Soon after reading this statement, he relinquished his huge wealth and walked out of his home in a single loincloth. The verse he read kindled the fire in his mind and made him realize the mortality of life and forced him to become a real ascetic. This power of theism is expressed by saint Thiruvalluvar as follows:

> Catch hold of the supreme power, which has no desire, to relinquish the desire in your mind.

> (Verse 350)

Let us have a closer look at this Thirukkural verse. An examination of the words in this verse will reveal many facts about the power of theism. The only way to relinquish our attachment to the materialistic world is to adhere to the supreme power which has total detachment. We may wonder about this advice. What is it, to attain detachment is advisable to get attached to something. Yes, it is essential to adhere to the almighty, which is free of desire, since this power has the power to relieve us of all the attraction towards land, money, and the opposite sex. As per theism, the desire to adhere to the almighty is the ambition to catch hold of the supreme power. This desire will cause only good effects meant for peaceful life. This desire is like the attachment of the ship sailing on water, without allowing the water to enter into it.

Theism is a sense related to the mind. That is why, this cannot be taught by an instructor or cannot be performed by others on our behalf. However, for those with built-in self-confidence, there is no need for the faith of theism to induce confidence, which is already there. But this kind of mind with built-in confidence is only in a very few in the world. Because of this nature, the religious principles proposed by sages are still alive and active all over the world. If all people in the world attain the level of gaining self-confidence on their own, then all religions in the world would cease to exist.

But the present state of the world is that almost all people, at some stage of their life, need the support of theism faith, like the help of the mother required for a tender child. Here comes a confusion because the theistic faith of different religions is not identical. For some, a glimpse of this faith is enough to inculcate confidence and make them progress in life. For some, this faith is analogous to the thorned stick required for making the bulls used to plough a farm field. These kinds of people are those without even a trace of self-confidence. The ignorance of this group of people is the capital for the priests who make their survival in the name of rituals. This kind of situation of keeping a cross section of the weak-minded population is the play of nature, since nature is aware of the fact that existence of ups and downs is the key for the life cycle.

## 3.8 Believers' World

A major portion of the world population believes in the existence of God. It does not mean that a majority of people in the world have seen or felt the presence of God. Indeed, leaving a few per cent in this cross section, the rest do not even have the desire to understand the immense power potential of their mind. Most people are involved in the daily rigamarole of surviving and taking care of their daily needs. Because of the pressures and responsibilities in their lives, they live almost without any faith or balance in their mind.

People, who have read about the lives of the great saints of India, know that these saints believed in God in the form of fire (Lord Shiva) and in the form of dark cloud (Lord Vishnu). These people hope that their prayers will fetch them their materialistic needs. In many cultures, people offer gifts or tokens of gratitude to the deities they worship which can be seen as a method or bartering with God for your wishes or needs. Many are foolish enough to go to the extent of striking a deal with God, bargaining offerings as a token (symbol) of gratitude.

According to ancient texts, those who attained knowledge through meditation would also attain eternal pleasure, such as their heart is filled with happiness and they become speechless, and rest in peace forever, like Arunagirinathar. This kind of eternal peaceful state is referred to as true sainthood. These saints did not have any attachments to their bodies either. They could not feel natural sensations such as thirst, hunger, sleep, and the ageing of their body. That is, their mental state could enable them to conquer even the natural instincts.

There is no evidence that these saints did achieve great knowledge about the universe or God, as has been described in texts or in oral stories. Therefore, whatever the believers of God say are their own hypothesis or faith. Thus, the question about arresting the mind to attain eternal bliss is still an open question. If so, is there any possibility for a person to have complete control of their minds like the saints in these accounts did? To get the power to control the power of mind? The world has been striving hard to find an answer to this question, without any success so far. However, recent experiments and scientific reports about the waves shed by mind offer us a deeper glimpse into these mysteries. Jim Robbins writes:

> The EEG (electroencephalograph) measures brainwaves of different frequencies within the brain. Electrodes are placed on specific sites on the scalp to detect and record the electrical impulses within the brain. A frequency is the number of times a wave repeats itself within a second. It can be compared to the frequencies that you tune into on your radio. If any of these frequencies are deficient, excessive, or difficult to access our mental performance can suffer. The raw EEG has usually been described in terms of frequency bands: Gamma greater than 30(Hz) BETA (13–30Hz),

ALPHA (8–12 Hz), THETA (4–8 Hz), and DELTA (less than 4 Hz. For example: "Our brain uses 13Hz (high alpha or low beta)) for "active" intelligence. Often we find individuals who exhibit learning disabilities and attention problems having a deficiency of 13Hz activity in certain brain regions that affects the ability to easily perform sequencing tasks and math calculations".

(Robbins, 2008)

The next question that comes to our mind is—is there no answer to this question? The human mind looks for something to hold on theism and atheism, they are some of the beliefs which it decides to cling to for a sense purpose, belonging, identity, peace and happiness, etc.

It is also true that both spiritual and atheist minds can lose their grip on their faith at times. When something which is not to its liking, such as poverty, old age, which result in an inability to do things as one does at youth and with wealth, it is natural that the grip the mind has on your faith, beliefs, and dogmas will be shaken up. The mind which remains stable even during such events is a real stable mind, which has the power to handle any situation. But it is also natural that the body equipped with such a powerful mind would adjust to the process of ageing and so on.

Finally, an important note on the effect of ageing on mind power. The nature teaches the world that anything that begins must also end. In accordance with nature's rule, anything that evolves as young should go through ageing process. This process in accordance with science will make the brain also to acquire power steadily with ageing, attain peak power at a certain age, and then its power would begin to decrease. A common example for this kind of natural process is the rise and fall of the *sun*. Though this happens owing to the movement of earth, the relative motion of sun shows that it rises in the dawn, reaches the peak of zenith, and then gradually comes down and sets in the dusk.

Although it is natural for the brainpower to decline with ageing, there are exceptions to this natural rule. This reiterates that the law of nature that governs the events of the universe is not directly applicable to the brain. This establishes the fact that brain is a black box and the science is yet to explore its full potential. Though science keeps probing into the governing principle of brainpower, it is yet to see the light. This may be regarded as the supremacy of nature which keeps warning the world that its power is beyond human perception.

## 3.9 Faith of Theists

The faith of mind which believes that God is responsible for all the events taking place is reflected as *theism*. The wisdom waves (*brain waves are, essentially, the evidence of electrical activity produced by your brain. When a group of neurons sends a burst of electrical pulses to another group of neurons, it creates a wave-like pattern. These waves are measured in speed cycles per second, which we describe as Hertz (Hz). Depending on how awake and alert you are, the waves might be very fast, or they might be very slow. They can and do change, based on what you're doing and how you're feeling)* emitted by this kind of mind also have quantity and quality. This fact can be compared with the theory of thermodynamics, which states that energy has both quantity and quality. The waves emitted by a mind are dictated by the volume flow rate and pressure of the blood that is circulated in its nerves system. For a human body, up to 40 years of age, the volume flow rate and pressure of the blood pumped by the heart will be significant, and both will gradually subside as the age advances. Thus, it is natural that up to 40 years of age, the force and quantity of blood flowing in the brain nerves will be higher than in those beyond 40 years of age. Because of this, the frequency and amplitude of the waves emitted by the mind in a young body will be higher than those emitted by the mind when the body becomes old.

## 3.10  Disciplining the Mind

How do you discipline the mind to act and achieve the things you desire? Is it easier or harder to curb emotional responses and calm the mind when you are younger or older? That the mind is capable of greater thinking ability when young is quite evident, but is it also harder to achieve the calm which is required to put it to good work? If we analyse the mind of Saint Arunagiri, who wrote one of the greatest literatures of Tamil language, *Thiruppugazh*, we will understand the power of disciplining the mind. After losing his health, he decided to go on a different path, he repented for his bad deeds, he composed the unparalleled great verses of *Thiruppugazh* (Arunagirinathar, 1986), which are regarded as one of greatest literatures of Tamil language. These results reveal that even though the mind of Arunagiri had an immense power, the power was composed of both bad and good. He eventually allowed the good to suppress his bad instincts and impulses as he became older and he was able to share his wisdom with the world through his works.

The evidence of power of the good and bad is clear from his composition which has two parts. The first part of all his poems describes the vigour of youth, the uninhibited instincts and desires this young mind possesses, and the actions which lead to ruin and decay. The second half presents the reversal of mind to noble path, the realization of God, and faith. To be precise, the first half of most of the verses of *Thiruppugazh* presents the sexual urge of his body and the associated disaster his body faced during his youth, and the second half narrates how his mind cleared during his old age and made him live a more nobler life.

Similar to the mind of Arunagiri, which possessed immense power potential, was that of Saint Thirunavukkarasar, a devotee of Lord Shiva, who lived in Tamil Nadu. He relinquished his Shaiva cult and joined Jainism (a religion which does not believe in idol worship). He then fiercely preached against Shaiva cult. But when he became old, he, returned to the Shaiva cult, and started doing social work, besides composing thousands of noble verses in Tamil. The collection of his songs is popularly known as *Devaram*, meaning poetic floral garland to God.

From Thirunavukkarasar's writings, we find out that he wanted to gain fame and recognition in his youth. He decided to follow Jainism to be more well known and for patronage. However, when he relinquished the faith, he had to face the ire and opposition of Emperor Mahendra Pallavan, the ruler of the southern part of India, with Kanchipuram as the capital. But Thiruna-vukkarasar's conviction in his belief in the Shaiva cult was strong enough to make the emperor to relinquish Jainism and follow the Shaiva cult. The two wrote wonderful poetry which is read even today by many. These writing and the lives of these saints emphasize both the presence of good and bad in every human mind and the need for discipline, and developing your own morality based on life experiences and rational thinking. Having conviction in your morality and beliefs has the power potential of the great mind of Thirunavukkarasar is evident from the verses of *Devaram* he composed. The life history of these two saints reveals that their mind had power to win over enmity of any order.

## Notes

1  Chapman Cohen, *Theism or Atheism the Great Alternative*, Tredition Classics, 2013.
2  Two of the most well-known Siddhars were Ramana Maharishi who passed away in 1950 and Vallal Ramalinga Swami who disappeared at the end of 19th century in India.

# 4 The Push and Pull of Science and Spirituality

## 4.1 Introduction

In the perception of the author, it may be speculated that the mind is a special intellectual machine that is capable of emitting thought waves of a mixed nature. If we try and classify this mixed wave spectrum, it may broadly be classified as bands of scientific and spiritual waves. The waves which are logic based and can be verified or proved may be regarded as scientific waves and those which are purely abstract and only may be felt and cannot be verified by physical means may be termed spiritual waves. When the spiritual waves emitted by a mind is dominant, the mind has a spiritual bent; and when the scientific waves emitted by a mind is dominant, the mind has a scientific bent. Human race always tries to explore and understand the quality and quantity of these waves with the aim of using them for the development of the world. Because of the immense power potential embedded in the mind, understanding it calls for some special practice based on immense thinking power. But so far there is only a partial success in this attempt by the scientists and spiritualists of the world.

The secrecy embedded in nature have many dimensions. Because of the complex nature, however great may be the power of a mind, it is almost impossible to gain a complete understanding of the secrecy of nature. Only due to this peculiar nature, a scientist enables him/her to understand, and catch up one or more in some cases, in the numerous branches of science, namely maths, physics, chemistry, biology, and so on, which are embedded in nature. The numerous scientific theories, postulations, and developments, which we have now, were the outcome of the capabilities of such powerful minds. People developed various application devices, used by the world, using the scientific principles invented by their theoretical minds. If a mind with a powerful scientific potential does not have a philosophical or spiritual side, it can be a disadvantage. But a mind with a blend of both will usually also possess great empathy and generosity since they realize that they are part of the vastness of the universe and, as Gandhi said, that humans are merely custodians of the wealth of the universe and not their owners.

DOI: 10.4324/9781003275527-4

Thus, however great may be the mind, only one which possesses a blend of the scientific and the spiritual will be able to achieve things for the greater good of humanity. The world has seen many cruel dictators, dangerous criminals, corrupt fellows, and persons with craze for power who do not care about anything but achieving their goals even at the cost of others and often exploiting and ruining the lives of other people. Similarly, a mind which has only a spiritual bent which does not give any precedence to logical/critical thinking and reasoning will practise spiritual exercises with a self-centred and hollow intention of having abstract happiness.

A mind which will make a person to dream not only about his happy life but also the happiness of the entire humanity will contain both scientific and spiritual energies since they will know not to be swayed by false promises of salvation in the name of God or religion and they are not likely to chase after arrogant fantasies of gaining immense power and wealth because they are capable of self-reflection. For a mind with both scientific and spiritual energies, if the (scientific) rational part is more overbearing than the spiritual, the person will make inventions and discoveries that are useful to the well-being of the world. Great scientists who shined in the scientific world, like Newton, Edison, and Einstein, were such people. The world will always celebrate their scientific contributions. A mind with both energies, where the spiritual is dominant, will never make a person to believe in superstition, in the name of spiritualism, and preach baseless hypotheses to the public. Instead, they will educate the world through their personal life. Thus, however great may be the power potential of a mind, only when there is balance will it have value in the world. At this stage, it is essential to note that all minds will have a blend of scientific and spiritual bent, only the proportion of these bents will vary from mind to mind. Dominance of these bents makes a person a scientist or spiritualist. That is, it may be stated that no mind is completely free from scientific or spiritual bent.

## 4.2 Ways to Control and Regulate the Mind

Is it possible to regulate the mind, let it lean towards being more scientific or rational or spiritualistic or philosophical? It is natural to have these kinds of questions. If it were possible to control the power of our mind, we could regulate it to an extent of achieving great things which will lift the entire world out of the many problems plaguing it.

People who have faith in the concept of God (Theists) believe that only with the grace of God can the mind be regulated and directed for doing good. They also firmly believe that without God's grace, it is impossible to control and regulate the mind power. In direct contrast to this faith, many believe that the power of nature, which is the controller of the universe, alone can regulate our mind and not God.

Theists believe that the faith in the concept of God has the power to regulate the mind. However, I believe that belief in God and religion also has the potential to suppress parts of our rational side, since faith in religion expects people to believe unconditionally without much question or criticism. While this is not universal, this theory holds true for many religious belief systems around the world.

At this stage, it may be helpful to consider that there also exists a principle such as conservation of energy for the mind power. This power has essentially two components: the scientific and spiritual. Therefore, a mind with spiritual component dominant is bound to have lesser scientific thinking, and vice versa. This nature can be observed in the life of many prominent persons like Einstein and Edison. In the words of Einstein, "Science without religion is lame, religion without science is blind" (The Guardian, Tue 13 May 2008) Albert Einstein and his famous aphorism have been the source of endless debate between believers and non-believers wanting to claim the greatest scientist of the 20th century as their own.

The quote of Einstein "Science without religion is lame, religion without science is blind" has been used to support the idea that Einstein was a religious man and a theist. This is a gross misrepresentation of what he meant. Einstein was not religious in any way, nor would he be considered a theist. He spoke of gods, and made reference to gods a few times but one must understand what he meant by the word "god" to clearly understand his point. Einstein could have been described as a Deist or a Pantheist. He acknowledged the existence of a power or set of rules that governed the behaviour of the universe, but he did not anthropomorphized it. Calling the mystical energy of the universe "God" is not in any way the same as calling the god of Christianity, Islam, Judaism, or any other religion "God".

The quote "science without religion is lame and religion without science is blind" by Einstein may be interpreted as follows. In the perception of the philosophers, god is a concept proposed by the founders of many religions to regulate humanity. Scientific theories and principles invented by scientists are for mostly materialistic benefits. We know that the materialistic comfort without peace of mind or the peace of mind without the basic materialistic comfort is of no value mainly to the human. Therefore, there should be an appropriate proportion of scientific and spiritual content in the mind to lead a comfortable life. This is what is conveyed by this famous quote of Einstein.

The effect of and extent of suppression of the scientific energy by the spiritual energy can clearly be inferred from the life of great scientists. Many ancient and modern scientists were atheists. For many scientists, who achieved the great feats, at a young age in their lives, their belief in the power of the mind was greater than their belief in the spiritual. This kind of change was clearly noticed in the life of Einstein [Result of WordNet Search for Einstein", 3.1. The Trustees of Princeton University, January 2015(2)] and Oppenheimer [Rouze, Michel, J. Robert Oppenheimer, Encyclopedia

Britannica. (16)]. In other words, often we observe that with age, people become more spiritual.

## 4.3 The Basis of Morality

In everyone's deed, good and bad will always prevail as this is the law of nature. This is common to all. This aspect has been nicely handled by Thiruvalluvar in his Thirukkural verse (Thiruvalluvar, 1986)

> Weighing well and good of each, his fallings clearly scan, as these or those prevail, so estimate the man.

> (Verse 504)

This simply means that we can consider a person's good qualities, as well as his faults, and then judge (of his character) by that which prevails. The inner substance of this great Thirukkural verse is that every person has both good and bad qualities. Thus, no one can be taken as a perfect character with good qualities only. Similarly, no one can be completely bad, without even the trace of good characters.

A farmer will carefully remove the weeds in the farmland in which he is cultivating the crop of his choice. Usually the farmer removes the weed right from its root. If we consider this superfluously, the farmer kills the living plants. But the intention here is to nurture the crop to make it grow well and to get a rich yield. Thus, essentially the farmer removes the hurdle in the form of weed, which stands in the way to make a healthy cultivation. Here the deed of the farmer in destroying the weed is a noble act.

Now, let us see an example which is directly opposed to the farmer's action. Let us consider a thief who robs money to fulfil his needs. Here the intention of the thief is to fulfil his need, but the way he adopts for satisfying his requirement is bad. Therefore, the act of the thief is considered not only bad, but also punishable. Thus, it is essential to consider both the action and the intention to judge whether the action is good or bad. The word "weigh" is so involved and it advises us to consider so many factors to judge a person.

The essence of this Thirukkural may be summarized as follows. The most important human endeavour is the striving for morality in our actions. Our inner balance and even our very existence depend on it. Only morality in our actions can give beauty and dignity to life. To make this a living force and bring it to clear consciousness is perhaps the foremost task of education.

Morality may also be viewed as code of values that directs man's choices and actions. It should be based on objective reality and empirical reason. Reason is the faculty by which man identifies and integrates the sensory input from the world, including what is good and what is bad for man. Reason discovers causal laws of nature, including moral principles to guide his course of action in life.

In simple language, it may be stated that a person with moral value is one whose words and deeds match. But this kind of perfection in human mind is next to impossible. Therefore, a mind possessing this measure of word–deed matching as the dominant and their mismatch is only a minor proportion can be regarded as noble. This is exactly the yardstick proposed by Thirukkural.

## 4.4 Variations in the Mind

If we take the age as *time* and experience as *space*, it can be stated that *the time and space rule the power of a mind.* This fact is clearly documented in one of the greatest grammatical literature books *Tholkappiam*, written in Tamil by Tholkappiar (Puliyur Kesigan, 2012).

It is well known that the energy level of body diminishes gradually with ageing. Owing to this effect, an experienced mind rarely gets excited. Even though there are exceptions to this state, such people are very few.

Thus, the age, namely the time, and space, namely the experience, have the power to regulate the mind and direct it. In other words, time and space are the two efficient teachers to train our mind to acquire a great level of wisdom. These two factors are powerful enough to control even the mind of great philosophers. Because of the power of time and space, only the mind of great saints, like Thirumoolar, Thiruvalluvar, Pattinathar, Thayumanavar, Ramakrishnar, Vallalar, Ramana Maharishi, as they had grown old realized that even prayer is a kind of attachment and stopped praying.

We can observe that this kind of detachment that occurs with ageing is common in nature too. For example, let us consider a mango tree. The tree will blossom at the beginning of the spring season for bearing fruits. The flowers will open up and tender mangoes will form. Some of the small ones will not have enough strength to hold on to the sting and fall down prematurely. But many of the tender mangoes will stick to the sting, grow, mature, and ripe. When they begin to ripe, their hold to the sting will loosen gradually. When fully ripened, the hold will totally go, and the fruit will come down and offer itself to the world. Many of us see these events every year. This episode demonstrates that the maturity leading to detachment is not unique to humans, but rather it is also common among species such as trees and plants. In the world of nature, some trees get hardened and become as hard as diamond, as they grow old. All these events reveal that time and space are the causes of maturity of all living things.

If we go a step further and observe the plant kingdom, it can be seen that after several seasons, some variety of trees become as hard as a granite rock. Indeed, scientists call these hardened trees as *stone trees.*

The power of science which is able to study and understand the atom, its energy potential, inner arrangements, and so on is so far unable to understand the reason behind the emission of energy waves from the minds of numerous living species. Even though scientists keep attempting to gain a grip and get a glimpse of this nature, it is yet to see the shore.

For the time being, we could rely on spiritualism and philosophy to take us closer to this mystery. It is unfortunate that the great saints who scaled this huge mountain become speechless the moment they reached the peak. Even we can encounter this kind of emotions. For example, if we succeed in an event that we aspire with a great expectation, our eyes would shed tears and we might not have words to express our joy. This kind of emotion can be observed in sports commonly. In great events such as the World Cup football, the team that wins the World Cup Final invariably goes extremely emotional to the extent of not even uttering a few words about his feeling to the press. Indeed, only after a gap, the press could be able to record their interview. Though this might appear as a simple example, it would convey the state attained by a mind after experiencing a great event.

The life and mind state of Bernard Shaw, who early on self-identified as an atheist (and always questioned organized religion) but in his later years put much thought into the possible existence of the divine, may be taken as an evidence for this change.

Atheist refers to someone who has no faith in god. Indeed, an atheist goes to the extent of not believing the words of a high-calibre person simply because he is a theist. Most atheists believe that having faith in god is a symptom of lack of self-confidence. The reason they cite for their argument against the philosophy of god is that if there is one such power, then why it is not visible. The reason for this kind of belief is that they mix up science and religion. For science, anything that is true should have some proof or verification. From this point of view, the argument of atheists may be taken as right. But there is the other side of the coin. For instance, the power of nature such as the potential of a magnetic field is not visible to our eyes and this does not mean that it does not exist. However, the world sees that a true atheist is one who believes firmly in his principle and never criticizes the theists.

## 4.5 Which Is Superior?

Just as the doubt about the existence or non-existence of God remains forever, the question which is superior among theism and atheism, and science and religion, remains an open question forever. It is extremely difficult to find an answer to this question. May be it can be concluded in this way. Superiority depends on the view and mindset of the persons who indulge in judging the attitude. In this way, it may be stated that both are equal and great in their own respect. For a mind with a scientific temper, science is superior. Similarly, for a mind with pure spiritual temper, spiritualism or theism is superior. These two faiths may be treated as our two eyes. Therefore, the question about the superiority of science and religion is something like asking which one is superior among our two eyes.

But if we study the lives of great scientists and saints, we can understand the following truth in the transition of mind from one faith to the other. Great scientists like Newton, Einstein, Oppenheimer, and Edison in their old age had a tendency to seek spiritualism. In the same manner, renowned saints, like Buddha, Mahavir, Vaishnava and Shaiva saints Arunagirinathar, Thayumanaver, Ramalinga Adigalar, Ramakrishna Paramahamsa, Vivekananda, and Kirupanandha Variyar, as they grew old curtailed their spiritual research and resorted to moving on the path of human service. At a mature age, they realized that "Service to Humanity is Service to God".

Thus, in both lifestyles, the firm path they follow at youth loosens gradually as the body grows old; in some cases, this event can take place suddenly too. This transition from one path to the other caused by age implies that the person's experiences in life and their observations about their environment has a greater hold on the mind of ageing body. Once we gain this understanding, we will realize that debate about the comparative merits of scientific and spirituality is meaningless.

From the accident met with by a cruel person, the medical world has begun its research to understand the brain, its nerve system, the characteristics of the waves emitted by it, and the consequences of its energy potential. But this research, though successful in giving a rough or a vague knowledge about the mind, is yet to go a long way to gain the complete understanding about this powerful device, which helps us gain an understanding of and think about science as well as spirituality. However, the limited knowledge gained itself is proved to be useful to the extent of curing some ailment to the brain and heart. On the heart side, the development is to the extent of replacing some of its parts with artificial ones.

Should there be a conflict between these two sects? A clear answer to this question is that this war is due to the fact that in reality, both these sects are just at the primitive stage of their faith. An atheist or a theist at a high level of their philosophy would not like to even debate on this. People at the highest plane of their philosophical faith are called those with "wide wisdom" by Tamil. These are the people who saw the width and depth of their faith, analysed the pros and cons of that, realized its expanse, engraved it in their mind module, and got illuminated. This calibre of balance is described as an extreme level of intelligence is ignorance by the student of Bernard Shaw.

The problem is not the belief itself but the conviction that whatever a holy text or a priest tells you is the holy word of a god and needs to be enforced no matter what the consequences. A theist's belief in a god does not harm anyone. A theist's conviction that his god finds homosexuality a sin and therefore gay people should not be allowed to marry or adopt children however does.

Atheism gives us one less reason to hurt other people. That's basically the only reason why an atheistic future might be better. But a theistic future where theists accept that their religion is a purely private matter and does not give them the right to make decisions for anyone but themselves might work just as well.

Atheism, per se, is not better than theism. Theism, however, makes people practice to adhere to concepts completely unsupported by evidences. While the specific belief in deities is not a motive for concerns, it teaches a person that not only believing in random things is normal, but also that it is actually good. On top of that, many times theism is accompanied by a set of immoral teachings. These things cause a detachment from reality that many times result in bigotry, prejudice, violence, and other immoral things. That is bad for our future (and consequently worse than atheism).

The bad thing is not atheism or theism. The bad thing is immorality. While the mere belief in a deity is not bad per se, it becomes bad when it discourages rationality and encourages immorality. Atheism doesn't suffer from that illness since, being contentless, cannot possibly discourage rationality or encourage any immorality.

## 4.6 Real Status of Other Faiths

If both theism and atheism are imaginary concepts, what is the real nature of the numerous faiths or sects such as astrology, psychology, meditation, palmistry, numerology, etc. which fascinate mankind? Are these hypotheses true or false? In spite of this basic doubt, we see that people follow these illusions like mad ones, all over the world. What could be the reason behind this blind following? Let us try to find an answer for this basic question from a neutral standpoint, with the help of human psychology.

We can analyse our mind and judge whether it is a powerful one or not. But we should note that this decision we make is not the final one. The proof for this uncertainty is that the formation of the brain system and its relationship to the mind power have not been understood by anyone so far.

The fact that we need to keep in mind is that both theism and atheism are equally good. Indeed, a real theist or atheist is one who not only will not hate the opposite faith but will also like and respect that. This kind of realization is the basis to judge a person as perfect in his faith. This kind balance will enable a person to make use of the full potential of the mind to serve all living species. A typical example of this kind of balanced mind is that of Saint Ramalinga Swami, which made him feel pain even when one-sense species of plant kingdom starves. Lord Buddha is another example of this kind of saint of great calibre. These saints, after attaining wisdom, did not show any symptoms of either theism or atheism. What was seen in their deeds was kindness and affection towards the world. In other words, it may be stated that a mind becomes above the concepts of theism and atheism, once the ignorance covering it is removed by the knowledge it gains by abstract or theoretical and applied aspects of education. Theoretical knowledge is that gained by formal education and the applied wisdom is that gained by experience of all kinds.

## 4.7  Is It Possible to Control and Change the Mind Power?

The question that might obviously come to our mind is that whether there is any means to modify, regulate, and control the mind power. This wonderful doubt is the capital for the numerous meditation schools, which have mushroomed everywhere. These schools coolly advertise that through meditation, your mind power can be enhanced. Power of the mind thus controlled can increase manifold. If you are a student, you can excel in your studies. If you are a grown-up person, the efficiency of your work skill will grow exponentially, thus the meditation we teach will change your mental state, enhance your talent, and make you shine like a bright star in life.

But here comes the hurdle. If meditation is the way to liberate our mind power, then we can strive hard to meditate and take the power of our mind to its peak. Having read about great saints who mastered the art of meditation, we know that these saints after reaching perennial peace were either not able to wake up from this state or were not able to speak. While we do not know the reasons why or how these seers reached this state, we can assume that the advertisements claiming that these schools will have people who are masters of meditation and spirituality are quite exaggerated to catch the attention of customers.

If so, does it mean that it is impossible to learn meditation? This question will naturally come to our mind. A firm answer to this question is a definite yes. If yes, how to learn that. First of all, we should realize that meditation is an exercise for the mind, hence related to its real state. This exercise is purely internal and solely personal. This cannot be taught by a teacher. If someone has to teach this exercise to our mind, the teacher should have the power to enter our mind and gain complete control over it. Now, it is sure that all of us realize the actual situation. In this situation, let us try to learn the means, which are purely personal and likely to empower our mind and lead us to real meditation.

Understanding how to control our mind begins with realizing that you are in full control of our state. Since our mind, body, and emotions are interconnected, we can use mind–body techniques to bring greater cognizance to our thinking, which in turn influences our feelings. The practice of embracing self-awareness in the current moment ultimately drives lasting happiness. In fact, research on self-determination theory demonstrates that the more we feel we are in control of our circumstances (by staying grounded in the moment), the more productive and fulfilled we are likely to feel.

## 4.8  Some Essential Points of Meditation

If we keenly observe and analyse the activities of real saints like the Buddhist monks, we will be surprised with the perfect control gained by them over the feelings such as hunger, anger, breathing, etc. with their intense meditation. They gain this kind of complete control over their feelings by training their mind through systematic and intense meditation. In this practice, a person should go through different stages in their meditation exercise. In this kind of meditation to gain complete control of the mind, while passing the stages of the exercise, the power of that stage will be felt by the mind. For instance, if one could succeed in controlling the anger, the immediate effect that will be flashed in the feeling is that a control that is not easy for a common man has been achieved. If the mind lingers around this pleasure, that might prove a hindrance to its progress to the next stage of higher control which may lead to a stage of getting rid of all kinds of emotions. Therefore, it is essential to ignore the pleasures that come to the mind at the success of each stage, for forging ahead to the higher stages. This kind of practice might have been the key for success of the great saints who attained wisdom. Buddha revealed the essence of this practice as "desire is the cause of misery".

### 4.8.1 Insensitive to the Present State

The first step in meditation is the practice to ignore the external attractions/disturbances such as noise, fragrances, comforts, taste, and observation. In short, this is a practice to make the body, mouth, eye, nose, and ear to get them elevated to a level to ignore their sense. Once this state is achieved, the next step in the meditation can be reached comfortably. In other words, it may be stated that the first step in the meditation that would lead to the control of organs is the vital step in the meditation practice. This calls for very intense practice such as that practised by Ramana Maharishi and Swami Vivekananda. With this basic understanding, let us proceed to the details of the stages in the meditation practice.

## 4.9 Steps to Learn Meditation

As the name implies, meditation is a state of eternal peace resulting in immense pleasure to our mind. This kind of pleasing state can only be achieved by intense exercise of our mind, focusing on controlling and regulating its thoughts. This is something like the pleasing amalgamation of a true couple. This can be realized only by personal internal exercise and an outsider cannot teach this.

Every mind has the potential to learn meditation, which is an intensive self-study of the highest order. Come on, let us try to think, study, analyse, and understand the steps in the path, which might lead us to practise meditation in a sequence.

Meditation is a kind of blessing that makes a mind get rid of all attachments. Some who has the capability to meditate is regarded as a person blessed by God. It may be stated that this kind of mind is the residence for peace. Because of this state, this kind of person becomes free from all disturbances, including ailment to the body. This condition would ensure that persons of this kind are successful in all their endeavours. If a person is scientist, he will be victorious in his field of research; if he is a prophet, his principles will be of such high calibre that they will attract the world to follow him. It may be stated that Buddha, Jesus Christ, and Prophet Mohammad were blessed with this kind of mind. From the principles promoted by these great saints, it may be inferred that the mind which has a complete control over the waves it sheds need to be devotional focusing on rituals and have bent towards serving the world. That is, great saints not only work for their spiritual elevation but also pray for the welfare of the world. It should be emphasized that service to the world for these saints is not restricted to humans alone but extends to all living things, beginning from one-sense plant kingdom to six-sense humans.

Another aspect to be underlined is that a mind of this kind of high calibre but with a scientific bent will also think of service to the world. Whatever be the bent, a mind that is successful in meditation will get its modules governing the realization, rational analysis, memory, etc. strengthened. In addition, meditation will also induce relaxation to both the body and mind leading to tranquillity. This is responsible for the regulation of even blood pressure.

Now the question that comes to our mind is that whether it is possible to practise meditation on our own or does it require some master for its learning. It is seen that meditation is a mind-related exercise. Therefore, it is natural to believe that if at all someone is capable to train a mind for meditation, then that instructor is expected to have the power to get into the mind which he attempts to train. But here comes another issue. It is known that each mind has its own characteristics and is totally different from other minds. This aspect about mind is something similar to the scientifically accepted fact about fingerprints signature, chemical constitution of hair, etc. Therefore, it is logical to think that it is not possible to impart mediation training to a mind by an instructor. If it is so, is there any means to learn meditation? This genuine question arises in our mind because we have seen that there were and are many saints and philosophers like Buddha, Ramana Maharishi, Ramakrishna Paramahamsa, Ramalinga Swamigal, Swami Vivekananda. The chapter on Meditation, which follows this chapter, addresses this vital and useful issue about meditation.

# 5  Meditation

## 5.1 Introduction

As we saw, meditation is purely an inner practice of our mind, and this practice is self-realization and no outsider can teach this to our mind (Eckhart Tolle, The Power of Now: A Guide to Spiritual Enlightenment, World Library, 2004). Therefore, meditation is essentially a self-education or practice to our mind. Also, it is to be kept in mind that it is an involved education demanding an immense effort blended with strong determination and tireless persistence. It is envisaged that there are basically four steps in the meditation exercise, as I have perceived. First of all, we should check whether our mind qualifies in the test to the first step. If qualified, we can move on to the second step, and so on. Let us see, in a simple manner, what are these steps.

### 5.1.1 First Step

Keen observation is the first step or stage or level of meditation exercise. The following is a simple test to study whether our mind has the power to observe keenly.

On a peak summer day, it is common to see that eagle soars in the sky without flocking. If we realize that this kind of simple and sustained soaring of the bird is because of the air thermal current that is established by the heated surface of the ground, then we can take it for granted that our mind has the power of observation. If our vision notices the scientific fact behind this natural event, then it can be taken that our mind has passed the preliminary text for the meditation course and it can comfortably move on to the second test. This test also reveals that this mind is one with scientific spirit. Your sense of observation can be tested in simple ways. Something as small as if on an exceptionally sunny day, you see someone reading in the evening hours. Suppose the person reading is sitting in front of a light such that the brightness from the light falls on the book from the front. If you ask the person to turn around and read so that the light will come from the rear and his eyes will not be strained, then you are observant enough to be able to perform meditation.

DOI: 10.4324/9781003275527-5

Being aware of your surrounding environment unconsciously proves that a person is conscientious and diligent; meditation or reflecting on the self will be a relatively easy exercise for these people.

### 5.1.2 Second Step

The mind that has keen observation should be tested for its ability to control its emotions. This is the second test in the meditation exercise. As a question for this second examination, let us consider that we are travelling, say walking, on a hot summer day. The summer heat will take away our energy and will force us to drink something, at least water to quench the thirst. This feeling is natural. Now, if your mind says that your destination is nearby, we need not look for water outside, instead we can drink water after reaching the place. If this command of the mind is accepted by your body, it implies that your mind and body have an understanding and they can work together. In case your body rejects the suggestion of the mind and remains adamant in searching for water before reaching the destination, the mind and body are not capable of working in synchronization. If you belong to the former category, you are eligible to move on to the third stage of meditation exercise.

### 5.1.3 Third Step

After ensuring that the body listens to and obeys the command of your mind, you can step on to the third stage. This third step is something special and has to be observed clearly and cautiously. A time which is convenient to us, say it is early morning, noon time, evening time, or late night, we should sit in a relaxed posture and try to make the brain relax and rest. In short, it may be taken as an effort to make the mind to move towards a peaceful state, without any exertion. For practising this stage, one needs to fix the time suitable for meditation, so that this exercise will not disturb his profession. If a mind that is qualified in the first two steps of meditation will be genuine to its profession and so will not allow a person to compromise on the duty and devote some for this stage of mediation practice. But judging the time suitable for the third stage practice will be easy for this kind of mind which worships its work.

For this practice, the surrounding environment should be congenial. This kind of environment is what is meant by suitable time for practising this involved step of meditation exercise. But when we try to calm the mind, its instantaneous reaction will be rebellious. We need not bother about this rebellious behaviour of our mind, since it is a natural animal reaction for our mind to jump out of the bound in which it is housed. But with practice, you will be able to focus on your surroundings and train your body and mind to work in synchronization, your mind will naturally have the power to control itself and refrain from drifting and achieve a sense of peace. It is only a question of time before you reach that end. For some people, this duration may be of a few days, for some others a few months, for some this time period may extend to as long as a few or several years.

Therefore, what we need to do is to try to keep the mind under control for as long a period as possible. On the first day, this exercise would be possible for a few seconds or few minutes only, and thereafter the mind will rush around and run in all directions. After a few days, you yourself will be surprised to note that the mind which was rebellious has become quite soft and cool to the extent of relaxing and resting for many minutes. After a few months, the relaxing duration will stretch to many hours, during which the mind will tend to move even to the state of eternal calm. This kind of tendency of the mind to transform gradually is an indication of attaining peace through meditation. Transiting gradually towards attaining total control of the emotions of the mind can be inferred from the ability to sit in a position for a long time which was not possible for us earlier, control our breathing from its normal rate to a very low rate, viewing the aesthetic beauty, and deriving immense pleasure from such view are the indication that our meditation bears the fruits that we aspired.

### 5.1.4 Fourth Step

The fourth step is a state which only those who have practised and dedicated their life to learning more about it can reach. It has been described as a state of eternal pleasure by saints. This is a state where the mind reaches heights which are above the celestial space. It enables the mind to relax, rest, and reside in eternal peace forever. Going by the ancient accounts (Thirumoolar, 1994), a mind which reaches this zenith of meditation sphere will acquire immense quantum of energy and limitless power to achieve anything it aspires to achieve. But the moment a mind attains this level, it will realize that all materialistic pleasures, including the pleasure of preaching, are momentary and will become silent. This is called the speechless state. Because of this, the saints who attained the highest state did not share their experience with the world. Saints like Ramalinga Swami, Vivekananda, and Thirumoolar are typical examples for people blessed with this kind of mind. After attaining wisdom, they did not give any advice to the world. But their lifestyle gave a galaxy of moral to the society. Therefore, it may be stated that though the mind of a person who gained perfect control over his mind goes speechless and unable to give any verbal message to the world, their deeds will be of very high calibre to the tune of imparting invaluable morals to the society.

Let us pray to God or nature to help us to meditate and get immersed in the practice of mediation and calming and training the mind. I am sure that an analysis, observation, inference, and practical experience can make us realize that meditation is purely a personal exercise of the highest order that cannot be learned from a teacher.

The extreme level of intelligence is ignorance. This statement describes the last state of meditation philosophically. In this statement, the "ignorance" signifies the state of total silence.

Thus, if we stimulate our mind to an extent of liberating the full potential embedded in it and use that power to meditate, according to accounts in various texts of religious philosophy and spiritual exercise, it is possible to cross these four stages and reach the peak. Immense practice with a single-minded devotion is required to qualify and reach the higher states of meditation.

I am sure that our discussion on meditation process has been somewhat confusing. Let us move further and try to understand the uses or benefits of meditation.

## 5.2  Benefits of Meditation

We hear that saints who mastered meditation lived long lives and were according to many accounts in a state of eternal peace and pleasure. While the descriptions are vague, we can try to understand what it might signify with the help of the following example from nature. Some saints of this calibre are Egyptian Christian saint Anthony (251–356), Italian Roman Catholic cardinal Corrado Bafile (1903–2005) (Rev. Alban Butler, "The Lives or the Fathers, Martyrs and Other Principal Saints" Vol. 1, 1864), and Italian Roman Catholic bishop Giovanni Benedetti (1917–2017).

We know that in places of high latitude, severe cold will prevail throughout the winter season. During this season, the earth surface will be covered with a very thick layer of snow. Because of this environment, most of the plants and trees will shed their leaves and stand as if dead in winter. This situation will lead to unavailability of food for the species living there. The species living in these places will eat a lot during spring and summer and accumulate lots of fat in their body, and will go to sleep when severe winter begins. During hibernation, these animals and birds will remain in a motionless state, like as if they are meditating. Because of this static state, what they need for their survival is a small amount of energy for the functioning of their heart to maintain the blood circulation. Owing to this, during hibernation, their body will become slightly thinner. Besides this change in their body, there won't be any other change in their system. Meditation could be described as being identical to hibernation. In the accounts mentioned previously, saints who meditate would breathe like us, about 12–20 times a minute. Instead, they may breathe only once in several minutes. Because of this, the quantum of oxygen provided by nature to their life will be preserved for a longer period than an ordinary person, according to Thirumandhiram.

Meditation involving breath control leads to longevity promotion. Control of breath makes the mind calm and this tranquillity of mind enhances the formation of reactive oxygen species (ROS). This process leads to control of stress. Reduced strain enables the organs function with ease and this kind of state results in increased longevity.

These facts *question Harman's Free Radical Theory of Ageing and rather suggest that ROS act as essential signalling molecules to promote metabolic health and longevity* (Ristow and Schmeisser, 2011).

That is why the saints could be able to have a longer life span than others. These saints usually prefer to live in a calm environment. Most of them would prefer to live in remote places such as deep forests and high mountain caves, without being spotted by the common public. Some of them are powerful enough to make their body invisible even. It is believed that this kind of invisible saints lives in Thiruvannamalai (a temple town in the northern part of Tamil Nadu, in India). One such saint was Tinnai Swami, who lived in the temple town Thiruvannamalai, in Tamil Nadu, India. He chose to live in isolation and invisible and led such a life till his end on December 7, 2003 (at the age of 91 years). In 1948, Tinnai Swami sought permission of Ramana Maharishi for migrating to Pondicherry, but Ramana Maharishi asked him to stay in Thriuvannamalai itself and wait. From then onwards, Tinnai Swami never left Tiruvannamalai and remained in the belief that he will go to the heaven.

Michael James[1] said, "though he remained most invisible to common man, I am fortunate enough to personally experience his grace".

Tinnai Swami maintained eternal silence, he did not express anything in writing too. The life of this saint conveys that the power of the mind of saints like him is powerful enough to shed waves that could convey many morals which cannot be conveyed by normal oral and written means.

Thus, meditation may be taken as the power of mind capable of controlling the body completely to the tune of even making it invisible. Now, let us ask this question: can an outsider enter into your mind and control it? Because of this entanglement only, we have stated that meditation is purely a personal and an intensive exercise of extremely high intensity. After examining the first three steps and if we pass them successfully, we can dare to enter the fourth step. Friends, the first three steps themselves are tedious, but with focused attention, anyone with a powerful mind can possibly cross them and reach the fourth step, which is the final one in the meditation procedure and just in the proximity of the eternal peaceful environment. With a deterministic mind, we may reach this final stage of meditation and enter the state of eternal bliss.

Now, let us ask ourselves whether we need this. If we are convinced that we have the inclination towards achieving this state, then we can seek to enter this practice of meditation exercise. So far, we tried to study, analyse, and understand the power of the brain to the maximum probable extent of our capability. This exercise was also a result of our brain's power of rational thinking. Theists believe that the Supreme Power, namely the God, directs all the deeds; I believe it is simply our brain which drives all thoughts and action. Events which seem greater than ourselves are also driven by our mind, this fact is quite evident to those whose minds are calm and in their control. This has been described by saint Thirumoolar as "the soul is the God and the body in which it resides in the temple, and the mind which realizes this becomes the God" (Thirumoolar, 1994). Thus, there is enough scope in theistic philosophy to deem our mind as God.

## 5.3  Miraculous Power of Meditation

Meditation being an exercise that enables one to remain in silence, focusing the mind on the goal one aspires to attain helps to calm the mind. Calmness of the mind results in getting relieved of unwanted waviness and thus lead to reduced stress. This kind of exercise leads to focused attention which is the key for success in our ventures. It also helps you become stronger to negative emotions. Some of the specific benefits of meditation are the following.

### 5.3.1  Reduces Stress

The life of all successful person the human history has shown is the testimony for the statement "healthy mind is one of the prime causes for a healthy body". Healthy mind is the key to success. It may also be stated that a healthy mind will enable a person to focus on his venture with unperturbed state. As many of us know, any work done with unperturbed mind will be successful. The main reason for this kind of state that our energy level attained is the single-minded devotion. Throughout this book, we keep iterating that the mind should be controlled to think without any diversion in its thought process. For attaining this state, meditation and proper breathing are the essential exercise one needs to practice. These exercise calm down the mind. A calm mind would make the person to relax and relieve of any stress accumulated due to workload. This would lead to a healthy heart and such a heart can keep the blood pressure in a systematic and controlled level. Once the blood flow is regulated, the mind would also receive the optimal flow of blood circulation. Such a mind will ensure that the person not only becomes stress-free but also thinks sharply. Thus, meditation helps to be free from unwanted stress and strain and enable us proceed in a path of right perspective. This enables a person to become free of negative emotions.

### 5.3.2  Strengthens the Mind and Body

By calming the mind, the meditation enables a person to have a clear focus on all his deeds. This kind of calm mind would lead not only to proper focus with full concentration on any venture but also result in better self-control. Such a state of mind will also give a person an inner sense of peace in everyday life.

### 5.3.3 Leads to Better Sleep

A clam mind state due to the practice of meditation and breathing exercise makes a person to attain sound sleep. A sound sleep is an important feature for our health and peace. Thus, it may be stated, "meditation is the natural medicine for health".

### 5.3.4 Improves Immunity

It is the experience of many of us that meditation enables us get relieved of any stress caused by our lifestyle, professional load, unwanted emotions, overambitiousness, greed, and jealousy. Coming out of the stress can result in even healing a person from any illness, especially those aggravated by stress, such as asthma, depression, fatigue, and anxiety disorders, among many others.

### 5.3.5 Improves Fertility

It is widely known that stress is one of the factors that contribute to fertility problems, and since meditation reduces stress, by doing so it can increase fertility. A woman can improve the chance of getting pregnant by practising meditation. This is because meditation makes her more relaxed and self-aware, leaving her open to the new experience, and also gets her better prepared for being a mother by teaching her coping strategies.

### 5.3.6 Unique Features of Meditation

The essentials of spirituality can be realized through meditation. During meditation, one can realize the transition process taking place in the mind that stimulates the intellectual power in the brain that enables the person to get a feel about the capability of the mind. Once this capability is gained, it is possible to have total control over the mind power and focus on achieving the desired goal, be it scientific or spiritual. The spiritual power embedded in the brain is powerful enough to make a person think sharp and behave soft exhibiting the characters that deem a person as scientist or saint. Saints like Buddha, Swami Vivekananda, Ramakrishna Paramahamsa, Ramana Maharishi, and Ramalinga Vallalar, who showed the path of discipline and honesty to the humanity, were those who could stimulate the spiritual power module in their brain, through their intense meditation. The experience of these great people highlights that meditation can make us calm and quiet so that we can understand and follow the path to reach the destiny we aspire.

Meditation is the exercise that can set right all maladies and sins committed during the course of one's life provided it is practised through constant perseverance and continued effort.

Although meditation is not easy to practice in routine life, if it is practised it can enable us to achieve the goals we aspire. For example, for a spiritualist, the ultimate goal is to attain divine power. The very fact that saints like Buddha attained this power is the testimony for the power of meditation. In the same manner, the achievement of great scientists across the world has been the result of their intense effort with single-minded devotion, which can be deemed as meditation. Meditation and spirituality bring about an unusual transformation in the quality of life, particularly that of mind, in case the practice is consistently done. These two aspects can liberate humanity from the undesirable earthly bondages and agonies of life due to which the mind, body, and soul lead to a distorted set-up of normal life.

## 5.4  Experience of Buddha

In all the regions of the world, it is believed that the founders of meditation were superhuman capable of performing miracles, which are not possible for a common man. But in the case of Buddha, the power surfaced is not through miracles but in a different form. Being a prince, he lived in comfort at his early age. But his mind was urging him to realize the truth of life. When he got a chance to see the world, he was shocked to learn that life is not the same for all. Some live in comfort and some suffer. This observation urged his mind to find the reason for this difference in the lifestyle. Many religious sects assign the reason for these as their fate and the consequence of the accumulation of the effects of good and bad deeds in the previous birth. This philosophy demands belief in rebirth theory. But Buddha questioned this theory. This question made his mind to think about the possibility of rebirth. He could not come out with any convincing conclusion about the theory of rebirth. Therefore, instead of pondering about something like the rebirth that has no definite proof, he began his search for the cause of suffering of humanity. His intense thought process and persisted single-minded devotion towards his search enlightened him with the truth about the sufferings of humankind. The wisdom he gained revealed him that "Desire is the cause of misery". Desire is the genesis for all the sufferings of human. The world has a mixture of good and bad. He realized that relinquishing the desire is the only means to come out of the sufferings. Also, there is no point in thinking about the existence of god, since no one is sure about its existence. Though many religious theories hypothesize that god is a divine power who can only be experienced and cannot be seen. Buddha did not get into this tussle about the existence or non-existence of god. His conviction was that instead of thinking about this abstract concept, it is wise to think of worldly endeavours. He lived in normal way. He did not believe in performing any miracle to show his divine power. Buddha was of the conviction that the power to perform miracle can be acquired through intense meditation. However, he was of the opinion that this kind of miracles is not meant for mesmerizing the public. Due to this principle, he advised his disciples not to exhibit their power, instead use them to serve the humanity. What he meant as miracles is the ability to walk on water, raise a dead, thought reading, fortune telling, and so on.

The following hearsay story tells us about the practical way of Buddha. One day Buddha met an ascetic near a river. The ascetic was very proud of the power he had developed by his intense practice for over 25 years. Buddha asked him what is that power. The ascetic said that with his miraculous power, he could walk over the water and cross the river. Buddha laughed and uttered what is the use of this power; the river can be crossed using a ferry for one penny! The reason behind this preaching of Buddha is that gaining miraculous power alone might tempt a person to misuse it (Buddhist Study and Practice Group).

*In countries following Buddhism, the saints mainly involve in imparting peace and kindness to humanity. Because of this practice, the people of these countries are not only well-educated but also have disciplined behaviour. This kind of culture is learnt by the public from the simple and holistic lifestyle of the monks. Among the Buddhists, the sect that follows Zen Buddhism is considered the group of the highest esteem, in terms of mind control and mental purity.*

*Like Buddhism, there are many other religions that preach and practice principles of high calibre and the priests and saints of these religions impart culture to ensure amenity in the society through their way of life. Indeed, these mind control practice of the saints of all religions are solely responsible for the tranquillity and peace of the world. Some of the well-known religions which can be quoted as examples for this calibre are the Islam, Christianity, Shintoism, Hinduism, Jainism, and others.*

## 5.5 Final Note

In the view of the author, meditation may be described as a means to make the mind calm so that it may think calmly. As we know, clam environment is the key to peace and happiness. This is true for the mind also. When it calms down, it gets immersed in happiness. Happiness is the state which makes the heart to beat normally, the blood circulation to become optimum, breathing rate to become even less than the normal breathing rate. Normal heart beat, proper blood circulation, and optimal breathing rate are the indication of a healthy body. Thus, the meditation exercise may be regarded as a practice to live healthy.

Meditation is essentially an inner exercise of high intensity and extreme focus to control and regulate the waves shed by the mind. Once gained, this kind of control over the mind can sail the person safe to the shore of the ocean he desired to reach. In addition to his safe sailing, a person with perfect control over his mind power would acquire the power and ability to make people adhere to the principles he practices and imparts to them.

Meditation is the state of doing nothing and letting go of all efforts to relax in our true nature, which is love, joy, and peace. Meditation gives us deep rest. It is essential to reduce stress levels and maintain mental hygiene.

Basically meditation calms the mind. A calm mind will be relieved of anything it wants to get rid of. This is the state desired not only by the saints but also by scientists aspiring to focus on their research. Another aspect is that meditation resulting in a calm mind can lead to regulated breathing also, which might be taken as a benefit from the health point of view.

For peace of mind, we need to stimulate the power embedded in our mind to use that power to control the emotional waves it could shed. Once this control is attained, we become relaxed and our heart beat becomes normal and our body becomes stress-free. These are the requirements for a healthy life. Thus, it may be stated that meditation is the key for keeping us fit and healthy.

Finally, the important fact we should keep in mind before venturing into learning or practising meditation is that being a self-exercise, it should be practised by ourselves. If we have this conviction and strong will, we can practise meditation to elevate our mind to liberate its potential to a large extent and excel in any task we undertake, without wasting our material wealth to someone, with the faith that he/she can train our mind to involve in meditation.

*The most common superpowers, which are believed to be linked with meditation practice, are the following. For saints, performing miracles which are not possible for a common man, such as reading the mind of others, predicting the future, self-healing and healing the diseases of others, and so on, is perceived to be the power of meditation. For scientists, it is the ability to focus on their work meant for development, discovery, and invention with single-minded devotion, without any perturbation of tiredness till the goal is reached. The world keeps witnessing the example of both these events throughout its history.*

## Note

1  www.arunachalasamudra.org/tinnaiswami.html, https://arunachalagrace.blogspot.com/search/label/invisible%20saint?m=0

# 6  Philosophy of Fate

## 6.1 Introduction

Theists believe that for every life, its journey from birth to end is devised by the supreme power of God. This is usually referred to as fate or destiny. They also believe in good or bad fate. Good fate brings fortune and bad fate brings misfortune. And both are believed to have a powerful hold on the lives of people.

Fate is commonly perceived as the effects of our deeds in the previous births that might affect us. The effect will be good and favourable if our deeds were good and adversely affect us if our deeds were bad. However, we cannot have any control on these effects, they will take their own course.

According to philosophy, destiny or fate is something that cannot be changed for it is governed by a supreme power and so each of our destinies is predetermined or fixed which is more of a concept of belief of the universe. Philosophy says that fortune tellers can study destiny.

Destiny is something which is fixed, and events taking place in our life is accordingly based on this fixed timeline. The obtaining of this knowledge is divination. Often this concept is misunderstood as fortune telling may be soothing initially, but when the actual problem arises, this philosophy may sound fatal which does not square with truth and reality.

All those who do not believe in themselves will resign their fate to the supreme power for the cause of events happening in their life instead of fighting it with courage and responsibility. The Universal Law of Harmony, Karma, defines that for every action there is an appropriate reaction and that no one can escape from it but have to face the consequences. But this doesn't mean that we can never come out of this; through right attitude and right effort, we can surely overcome it.

Man is unique among all the living beings of the universe because of his principle of mind. It is this principle that makes him unique for he is solely responsible for all his deeds. Man has to be discriminate in whatever he is doing for he has to make moral choices in choosing the right or the wrong thing to proceed with. Once he has decided to proceed his journey in the

DOI: 10.4324/9781003275527-6

direction he has opted for, then he becomes responsible for the consequences and have to face it whether it is sorrow or happiness. This is what is called karma and in this journey to our destiny, we also learn the lessons of life.

What does it mean to believe in fate? To believe in fate is to believe that there are now truths about all of the future actions that any of us will undertake. So, for example, if fate is real, then it is already true now that you will marry a certain person. Or, to pick a more grim example, there is already a truth about the exact moment you will die and how.

Thiruvalluvar, the Tamil poet, describes the power of fate in one of his verses (Thiruvalluvar, 1986):

> There is no match to the power of fate, and it would push aside whatever surrounds it and march forward.
>
> (Verse 380)

Believers in fate or destiny believe that it is powerful enough to push aside whatever surrounds it, including individual action, agency, and prayers. It bulldozes good and bad intentions and marches ahead. If we run with this definition of fate, can we say that it contradicts our rational thought and action? If we believe that our brain, logic, and reason determine our actions and futures, does fate or any notion of pre-destiny not run counter to this argument? And is the belief in fate not irrational or a superstition? In the following paragraphs, we will examine the definition and philosophical justifications behind the belief in fate, and how it is linked very intrinsically with the mind, its power, and human agency.

Societies in various parts of the world have had belief in fate, it is called in various ways in different languages, The ubiquitousness of this idea and the power it wields on peoples' lives have to be investigated. Why do many people believe that their thoughts and actions are a by-product of fate which will set them aside and lead their life in the path devised by it. If we believe that fate does hold power over human lives, it is natural to ask next: is it impossible to win over it or defeat it? Thirukkural (Thiruvalluvar, 1986) says that it is possible. The verse conveys the message in this way:

> Those who forge ahead without tiredness in their journey to their destination will push back the fate and move forward.
>
> (Verse 620)

This verse ascertains that fate can be conquered by tireless efforts. The importance of effort and human agency can be found in many ancient texts like Thiruvalluvar's, many verses of Sangam Literature of Tamil, statements such as "devotion to duty"; it means to fulfil your obligations—professional, legal, and moral. Accept responsibility for your own actions and those entrusted to your care. The argument that the human mind is bigger than the mysterious powers of the universe, God, or nature can be found in our literature and history from the beginning of time. Many notable thinkers and philosophers have laid emphasis on the power of the mind over its surroundings.

Einstein addresses this aspect as follows:

> I'm not an atheist, and I don't think I can call myself a pantheist. We are in the position of a little child entering a huge library filled with books in many languages. The child knows someone must have written those books. It does not know how. It does not understand the languages in which they are written. The child dimly suspects a mysterious order in the arrangement of the books but doesn't know what it is. That is, it seems to me, is the attitude of even the most intelligent human being toward God. We see the universe marvelously arranged and obeying certain laws but only dimly understand these laws. Our limited minds grasp the mysterious force that moves the constellations.
>
> (Letters to Solovine, Philosophical Library, 1987, p. 131)

Here comes an important issue. How to find out whether we can go against fate or destiny? Does the human mind have the power for this kind of effort? To find out whether we have such a power to forge ahead, what we need to do is perform self-examination.

## 6.2  Self-reflection

Self-reflection or introspection is a difficult but essential task which all human beings should be well-versed in. Self-reflection allows us to not only be more aware of our limitations and failures but also equips us with the knowledge about our mind and behaviour in order to learn and teach ourselves to do well. When challenged with an immovable force, a person who has learned to self-reflect will, while being aware of their strengths and limitations, make a concerted effort to win over the challenges. The term self-reflection denotes the act or state of being reflected, while introspection has to do with the observation or examination of one's own mental and emotional state of mind.

Age is immaterial for self-reflection. If we look back at the path we have travelled so far, with a focused attention, we will be able to learn more about ourselves and our relationship with our surroundings. It takes focused attention to keep walking on the road which you are determined to travel and not drift or veer away from it in the face of distractions and events which are happening in our surroundings. It takes practised effort to reflect on ourselves and train our minds to adapt and take actions based on our strengths and limitations. To merely ignore or be unaffected by our surroundings is not enough. Only a mind which has learned to introspect can move forward against fate.

Our mind has to acclimate to the surroundings with great effort and push against fate to keep moving forward on your chosen path. Small and big events and disasters in our lives sometimes set us on a different road. But if you are able to adapt to and navigate that path and find your way back towards your goals and principles, you have the determination to push back at fate.

A typical example of this kind of event is the battle fought by emperor Babur, who invaded Kabul in spite of the warning given by his court astrologer, stating that the time for battle scheduled by the emperor was not favourable (Madhan, 2016). The reason why Babur was able to go against this time-honoured tradition of going with the astrologer's words is because he had complete confidence in his army and his own military abilities.[1]

Therefore, fate might be taken as the war between our brain and our surroundings. In this war, if our mind wins, we can push fate aside and travel on our path to achieve our ambitions. If the surroundings overpower the brain, the person will follow his fate and depending on its nature will end up in either a good or a bad destination.

Fate is described by many as something immovable as an engraving on our skull by God, and by astrologers as something which is determined by the good and bad deeds in our previous births. This definition is nothing but humbug. Presuming that we have this understanding about the hypothesis of fate, let us now examine whether our brain has the power to conquer, control, and regulate itself through self-reflection.

Self-realization is discerning the nature of our wisdom or mind power; in other words, probing into our mind with the aim of estimating its potential power to analyse and come out with the fact about something that we would like to learn or understand. It we are successful in this analysis and ensure that our mind is capable of performing a task we would like to undertake, it implies that we have a realization about the power potential of our mind. This realization plays a dominant role in our life since life of all of us revolves around the process that our mind is capable of. A simple example might elaborate the meaning of self-realization. We see gold in various shapes as ornaments, but the metal used to make these are simply the metal gold. A mind with deep sense will see all the jewels as gold, but a mind with superficial sense of thinking will focus only on the shapes and design and enjoy the beauty of the ornaments. However, it should be noted that a mind is equipped with both these views. It is the state of the person and the circumstances that activate the view angle.

### 6.2.1 *What Is That We Realize?*

A mind capable of realizing the origin of any object or event is a power. Such a mind is capable of seeing, say, energy is something beyond what we perceive. For example, a common man will see diesel as a fuel meant for internal combustion engine. But a scientific mind capable of deep thinking will see diesel as a hydrocarbon compound possessing high calorific value and the energy contained in it that can be liberated. In both these views, the basic underlying fact is that diesel is a fuel, but the former mind realizes it as just a fuel and the latter mind views it as a compound made up of many scientific features.

The moment we are able to see this energy, which is beyond this physical form, we are realized. So, what is it that we realize? We realize that we are not the body, we are not the mind, but we are indeed the life energy. The life energy is immortal; it never dies, as per the eastern philosophy. The body dies and disintegrates, but the life energy, the Soul or the Spirit, can merge with the Universal Soul on self-realization. Self-realization further leads to God realization, which is a journey of realizing the truth about God and thus knowing God—the relationship between God and man. This spiritual awakening is the path to eternal happiness, peace, and bliss, leading us to our ultimate destination—Liberation or Enlightenment.

Being spiritually awake means knowing yourself and your true potential while being in your higher consciousness and deeper mental awareness. The degree of freedom from the unwanted thoughts and the degree of concentration on a single thought are the measures to gauge Enlightenment. For this we need to liberate our mind to become totally free from doubts. For attaining this state, the only way is to erase the module in the thinking that is the origin for doubts. Therefore, achieving this high-level doubts-free state is to realize that doubts never end. If one doubt is removed, another takes its place. It is like removing the leaves of a tree one by one. Even if all the leaves are clipped off, new ones grow. The tree itself must be uprooted.

## 6.3 Brain and Intention

Saints and philosophers, who tried to examine and understand the mind, found the depth of the topic of unimaginable magnitude. Let us try and analyse this problem, which is so deep, with a firm belief that we will be successful in deciphering it. From a psychological point of view, the faith that we have will take us to a very long distance and towards the goal post.

Let us try to understand the difference between mind and intention. As we know, the brain is the main controller of all the actions of the body in which it resides. That is, the brain is the supreme commander of the body. The structure of the brain has a complicated formation of nerves embedded in it. The power of the mind is dictated by the frequency and amplitude of the waves it emits. We know that these waves sometimes can exhibit an unexpected sudden peak in its amplitude. This kind of peak in the amplitude is a screech, something similar to the sudden spike in the frequency of the sound spectrum (Rathakrishnan, 2009). A mind capable of emitting waves with a screech peak is capable of devising many things that is commonly not possible. The scientific inventions the world has seen are due to this kind of waves only. Therefore, it may be stated that the mind of scientists, philosophers, and saints are equipped with this kind of power.

The power of Gandhi's mind was quite special. He realized the fact that the principle of non-violence and satyagraha are equivalent to salvation. He demonstrated the power of this principle by fighting the military might of the British Government without any weapons. His principles of non-violence and truth made him the leader of the masses. Gandhian philosophy places a lot of emphasis on truth and self-reflection, a moral and truthful person does not need the strength of guns and bullets to fight for their beliefs. Gandhi's philosophy and writings are read by many even today and he is celebrated as a leader of the people because his philosophy emphasizes the power of determination, truth, and the human mind.

On August 9, 1945, the United States dropped an atomic bomb on the city of Nagasaki, Japan, three days after bombing Hiroshima. By the end of 1945, an estimated 200,000 people had died in the two cities. Albert Einstein, upon hearing the news of the Hiroshima bombing, expressed sadness and regret. Although he never worked directly on the atomic bomb, Einstein is often incorrectly associated with the advent of nuclear weapons. His famous equation $E = mc^2$ explains the energy released in an atomic bomb but doesn't explain how to build one. He repeatedly reminded people that he did not consider himself the father of atomic energy. His part in it was quite indirect.

Einstein was disappointed when America tested the atom bomb. But when the US Airforce dropped atom bombs on Hiroshima and Nagasaki cities of Japan, at the end of the Second World War, the devastation caused by the bombs broke Einstein's heart. He was very much dejected and in agony. While in this state, he wrote a letter to Mahatma Gandhi expressing his feelings and conveyed that if he had known that his energy equation would be used for making weapons of mass destruction such as the atomic bomb, he would not have invented it. He tendered his apology to the world for the mistake he had committed by publishing the energy relation. It is believed that this letter from Einstein to Mahatma Gandhi is preserved in the Gandhi Museum in the city of Dehradun, in the northern part of India.

The intention to do good and be honest are qualities that minds of great leaders, humanitarians, and scientists possess, the intention to do good to society and remain true to their conscience. These features of a noble mind are reflected in the words and deeds of great personalities. Noble people, through their practice of self-reflection and assessment, strive hard to achieve this mind state.

Contemplating on the power of the mind is both a scientific and philosophical exercise. Discussing the mysteries of the mind often creates more confusion than understanding. In all fairness, we must accept this fact. If our mind has the maturity to accept this bare truth, it can be taken for granted that we have the potential to venture into this complicated analysis with extreme caution and understand some more facts about the treasure embedded in the mind.

We used analogies from theories of physics such as thermodynamics, heat transfer, and quantum mechanics in our study of the mind. These analogies complement our arguments about mind power, since the evolution and birth of these three branches of science clearly present that there is always scope for something better than what the mind envisages. Thus, the purpose of seeking the assistance of these sciences is only to gain some understanding about the power of the powerful, but least understood power centre, the mind, and not aiming at gaining total clarity about the potential of the mind. If our mind feels that it does not have the potential to scale the power mountain of mind, it means that our mind is a high-calibre device, commented by William Shakespeare; a fool does think he is wise but a wise man knows himself to be a fool (Shakespeare, 1966). This fact has been explicitly stated, in a philosophical manner, by the disciple of Bernard Shaw as "He who realizes himself as a fool will be listed at the top of the list of intellectuals". The inner current of this statement is that a mind which has the power to probe itself will realize its ignorance first. This kind of realization will clear its ignorance and make its intelligence to shine like a star.

The same fact has been narrated by saint Thiruvalluvar as follows:

Water will seep out from the river bed once the sand covering it is removed, in the same manner the wisdom of a person will surface once the ignorance covering it is cleared with education.

(Verse 396)

The deeper meaning of this wonderful verse is the following: wisdom is not alien to a mind. But the limitless wisdom of the mind is masked by the ignorance covering it, like the sand covering the water current in a riverbed. Like the water that seeps out when the sand is removed, the wisdom will shine when the ignorance is removed.

This message of Thirukkural has been stated in a different way by the disciple of Bernard Shaw. Please look at the verse carefully. What the Thirukkural says is that education or study will remove ignorance. The word used is education and not reading. Reading is different from studying. If we see something superficially, it is reading. If we see something deeply, fix it in our mind for productive application, the process is termed studying something. For instance, we read a story but learn a lesson. These statements come without our knowledge, depending on the context. For studying a subject, the mind devises a scheme which involves planning, execution, analysis, and retention. For this, the mind devotes a considerable portion of its power potential, whereas what a mind spends for reading a story is almost an insignificant amount of its power.

## 6.4 Intention

Intention may be considered a mental state behind doing something. That is why Mahatma Gandhi was of the opinion that it is not just the deed but also the motivation that should be considered to judge the quality of an action. In other words, it may be stated that the intention behind one's deeds is more important to judge a person. That is, the motive behind the deed is the basis for judging the calibre of that act. Let us describe a simple event that can be understood by anybody to clarify the power of intention. Say, at late night-time, a young couple is returning home after a function. The girl is wearing expensive ornaments. A group of bad elements surround them with the intention of robbing the jewels. When her husband tried to protect the girl, the bad group began to attack the young man. At that juncture, another person coming from the opposite direction noticed this. He was a courageous person knowing martial art. He became furious, attacked the bad elements, saved the young couple from the evil group, and safely sent them to their home. This deed was flashed in the morning newspapers as "noble act by a courageous person".

Now let us assume that the same young couple is returning home late night. A bad person with an intention of robbing their wealth approached them. When the husband resisted the act of the bad person, he attacked the husband and ran away with the jewels. Next day the newspapers flashed this news with the heading "a cruel criminal act of an evil man". When one person attacked a group, it was perceived as noble act and when one person was attacked, it is perceived as a criminal act, simply because the intention behind the former episode was saving a young couple and the intention behind the latter episode was stealing the jewels. This simple example explains the meaning of intention explicitly.

The principal task of the philosophy of intention is to uncover and describe the unity of motivation and deed. This project matters for not only questions of the philosophy of mind, but also the ethics of any deed executed with the philosophy. The intention behind any act executed may be noble or evil. The action gets the label of good or bad based on whether the intention behind that is noble or evil.

Intentions are responsible for the planning and execution of any action. Thus, the planning and execution are interlinked. That is, intention may be interpreted as the knowledge of the mind to perceive and implement an act.

The intention may also be interpreted as the capability of a mind to devise a plan and identify the ways to execute that plan at the appropriate time so that the deed will be successful. In many acts we encounter in our everyday life we can experience this. For example, if we plan to plant a seed, we first look for a quality seed and procure it. Then we select a soil suitable for that. Once these two stages are over, we look for the appropriate season to put the seed into the soil bed with suitable gaps between the seeds; we push the seeds gently into the soil so that they are at the required depth below the soil surface.

Then we gently spray water to establish the required humidity level for the seeds to germinate. Once these events are completed, we ensure that the soil receives enough sunshine so that the buds from the seeds will get the required energy to break the soil and come up. Once they come up, we protect them from insects and animals to ensure they grow and yield. In this execution, the intention behind the deed is manifold. Thus, the mind which plans something for execution is capable of devising the sequence events with proper judgement on the season, the environment, and other requirements to ensure that the plan is implemented successfully.

## Note

1   The Babur-nama in English (Memoirs of Babur). Translated from the original Turki Text by Byannette Susannah Beveridge. Issued in Four Fasciculi – Farghana 1912 – Kabul 1914 – Hindustan 1917 – Preface, Indices, etc. 1921. Vol. II, Sold by Luzac & co, 46, Great Russell Street, London.

# 7    Epilogue

In this book, we have tried our best to get a glimpse of the power potential of the mind, its spectral content, executive power, ways to stimulate, and release this power. We have explored theories about the limitlessness of our minds by using analogies and theories from science, philosophy, theology, nature, and even poetry. Many facts presented in this book are purely based on the intuition of the author. Wherever some quotes are present, their source and the authors are mentioned. Views from popular literature such as Thirukkural are the essence of the verses as perceived by the author. Throughout the book, the power potential embedded in the mind is analysed from scientific and philosophical viewpoints. Therefore, these views might appear hypothetical at some places. However, it is presumed that even the points which appear abstract will be of value not only to gain an understanding of the mind power but also in getting an idea to stimulate the mind to release its potential and use it for useful purposes.

Even though our mind is like a black box, human beings cannot help but try and explore and study its mysteries despite knowing that it is impossible to quantify its power. Philosophers, thinkers, and saints who have studied and written about the potential of the mind have all come to the same conclusion, but our attempts to understand it ourselves will never cease. In this book, we ventured into this formidable task simply because of the curiosity stemming from our minds, which has power not only over our body but also over our soul. From our intense study, we realized that the power of the mind might be tapped into with extraordinary efforts in understanding that the mind regulate its power mandatorily. It is certain that we will shine and acquire a special place in the society if we succeed in this Herculean task of stimulating our mind to release the power embedded in it to the maximum possible extent. Indeed, all high-calibre personalities the world celebrates are people who were successful in stimulating their mind and bringing out the mind power for executing their deeds. Another feature that must be kept in mind is that the meditation which is perceived as the means to control the mind and make it to release its power potential is a personal exercise and cannot be learnt from an instructor. Of course, sometimes learning a few aspects of meditation

DOI: 10.4324/9781003275527-7

might also will be of value to a few. But whatever is the means to learn the meditation, it is purely a self-exercise, and its success pins on the effort of the individual who aspires to learn it.

Self-control or willpower is something extremely difficult to acquire. Mahatma Gandhi narrated it as something which comes from within us and not from any external source. The world has seen that there were people blessed with the power to control their mind at birth itself, some gained this with intense mind exercise and some who could not gain it in spite of their intense effort. The first group is blessed people. Buddha and Jesus are typical example of this kind of people. Saints of the world as seen are examples of the group that acquired self-control with intense exercise.

The discussions presented in this book might help us to gain an understanding about the energy potential of our mind, to liberate it and use for productive actions, noble deeds, and scientific thinking of high calibre.

It will be of great value if we are able to gain control over the ways to regulate the energy potential of our mind. It is essential to realize that this exercise is hard but not impossible for a strong mind. If we reach this level, we will be in a perennial state of peace. If we firmly believe that we can gain control over our mind, that belief itself will take us to the right path leading to the destination. Therefore, let us have this kind of strong conviction before venturing into the exercise to understand our mind: devise the means suitable for our mind to liberate the energy embedded in it and use it for achieving the goal we aspire to achieve.

Those who worked hard and reached the foot of this unscalable mountain cannot express their feelings to society. Finally, a word of optimism. Let us believe that the facts, consequences, and the end results we have analysed, with the power of our mind, will raise us to the level of practising meditation, climbing all the four steps of it, and reaping the benefits of knowing ourselves better and the awareness and calm it brings with it.

# References

Alexander, C. N., E. J. Langer, R. I. Newman, H. M. Chandler and J. L. Davies, Tran-
scendental Meditation, Mindfulness, and Longevity: An Experimental Study with
the Elderly, *Journal of Personality and Social Psychology*, *57*(6), 1989, 950–964,
https://doi.org/10.1037/0022-3514.57.6.950.

Arunagirinathar, *Thiruppugaz*, Vanathi Pathippakam, 1986.

Biography of G.D. Naidu-Indian Scientist and Inventor, Posted 7 February 2013, https://
www.infoqueenbee.com/2013/02/biography-of-gdnaidu-indian-scientist.html.

Buddhist Study and Practice Group, www.sinc.sunysb.edu/Clubs/buddhism/.

Butler, Alban, *The Lives or the Fathers, Martyrs and Other Principal Saints*, vol. 1, 1864.

Chronister, Kim, *Peak Mindset: The New Science of Success*, CreateSpace Independent
Publishing Platform, 2017.

Cohen, Chapman, *Theism or Atheism the Great Alternative*, Tredition Classics, 2013.

Einstein, A., *Letters to Solovine*, Philosophical Library, 1987, p. 131.

Francis, W., Extract from page 316–317 of Madras District Gazetteers-South Arcot
District by W. Francis I.C.S., https://ramanisblog.in/2022/01/24/sage-dematrialized-
gazette-notification-1880.

Gosling, David L., *The Prophet of Modern India: A Biography of Swami Vivekananda*,
Rupa & Company, 2007.

Greene, John and Ian Bone, *Understanding Neurology—A Problem–Orientated
Approach: A Problem-Oriented Approach (Medical Understanding Series)*, Manson
Publishing Ltd., 2007.

Griffiths, David J. and Darrell F. Schroeter, *Introduction to Quantum Mechanics*, Cambridge University Press, 3rd ed., 2018.

The Guardian, Tue 13 May 2008, https://www.theguardian.com/theguardian/2008/
may/13.

Harlow, John, *The American Phrenological Journal and Repository of Science*, 1851
edition, Health News from National Public Radio, NPR, 2017.

James, Michael, www.arunachalasamudra.org/tinnaiswami.html, https://arunachala
grace.blogspot.com/search/label/invisible%20saint?m=0.

Madhan, *Vantharkal Vendrarkal*, Vikatan.com Private Ltd., 2016.

Murphy, Joseph, *The Power of Your Subconscious Mind*, Bantam, revised ed., 2001.

Natarajan, B., *"The Sage Thayumanavar- Voice of Thayumanavar the Silent Sage" Bio-
graphical Introduction*, Web Publication by Mountain Man Graphics, 1978.

Oppy, Graham and Pearce, Kenneth L., *Is There a God?* (Little Debates about Big Questions), Routledge, 1st ed., 13 October 2021.

Pepperell, Robert, Consciousness as a Physical Process Caused by the Organization of Energy in Brain, *Frontiers in Psychology*, 01 November 2018, http.//doi.org/10.3389/fpsyg.2018.02091.

Premji, Azim, Mahatma Gandhi's Idea of the Rich as Trustees Can Make an Effective, Sustainable Difference, *The Indian Express*, 2022.

Puliyur Kesigan, *Tholkappiar*, Paari Nilayam, 2nd ed., 2012.

Rathakrishnan, Ethirajan, Experimental Studies on the Limiting Tab, *AIAA Journal*, *47*(10), 2009, 2475–2485.

Rathakrishnan, Ethirajan, *Elements of Heat Transfer*, CRC Press, 2012.

Rathakrishnan, Ethirajan, *High Enthalpy Gas Dynamics*, Wiley, 2015.

Rathakrishnan, Ethirajan, *The Power of Spiritualism a Bi-lingual Book in Tamil and English*, Vanathi Pathippakam, 2021.

*Religion and Science, Stanford Encyclopedia of Philosophy Archive*, 17 January 2017.

Ristow, Michael and Sebastian Schmeisser, Extending Life Span by Increasing Oxidative Stress, *Free Radical Biology and Medicine*, *51*(2), 15 July 2011, 327–336, Epub 14 May 2011, https://doi.org/10.1016/j.freeradbiomed.2011.05.010.

Robbins, Jim, A *Symphony in the Brain: The Evolution of the New Brain Wave Biofeedback*, Grove Press, 2008.

Rouze, Michel and J. Robert Oppenheimer, *Encyclopedia Britannica*, 2023, https://www.britannica.com/biography/J-Robert-Oppenheimer.

Shakespeare, William, *As You Like It*, Cambridge university Press, 1966.

Thirumoolar, *Thirumandhiram*, The South Indian Saiva Siddhanta Works Publishing Society, Tinnevelly Ltd., vol. I, 1994.

Thiruvalluvar, *Thirukkural*, Poonpugaar Pathippagam, 1986.

Tolle, Eckhart, *The Power of Now: A Guide to Spiritual Enlightenment*, World Library, 2004.

The Trustees of Princeton University, January 2015, https://finance.princeton.edu/document/2666.

Zemanskey, Mark W., *Heat and Thermodynamics*, McGraw-Hill Book Company, 5th ed., 1968.

# Index

For Product Safety Concerns and Information please contact our EU
representative GPSR@taylorandfrancis.com
Taylor & Francis Verlag GmbH, Kaufingerstraße 24, 80331 München, Germany